SACRAMENTO PUBLIC LIBRARY

D0090715

Praise for *Disciplined Dreaming*

"It is often said there are dreamers and there are doers. Never before has someone connected the dots and clarified the path between 'dreaming' and 'doing' like Josh Linkner has in *Disciplined Dreaming*. This is a must-read for the innovators and creators who want to cross over to the execution side and make their dreams come to life."

> —**Dan Gilbert,** chairman and founder, Quicken Loans, and majority owner, Cleveland Cavaliers

"Creativity fuels the growth engine that drives results. *Disciplined Dreaming* gives us a practical and inspirational roadmap to move us from incremental improvements to radical breakthroughs. Josh Linkner has successfully built some of the most creative companies in the world and shows us the way."

> —**Jeff DeGraff,** professor, Ross School of Business, University of Michigan, Ann Arbor, and author, *Leading Innovation* and *Creativity at Work*

"Innovation in the workplace is what allows organizations to excel and exceed customer expectations. In this must-read book, Josh Linkner provides concrete ways to increase creativity within any business so it can grow and succeed in today's very competitive marketplace. *Disciplined Dreaming* provides fun and exciting ways to motivate both individuals and teams at all levels of any organization. Highly recommended!"

> —**Curt Avallone,** chief marketing officer, Sears

"Now all those days I spent dreaming can be put to good use. *Disciplined Dreaming* helps you harness your creativity. Well worth your time."

> —**Keith Crain,** chairman and CEO, Crain Communications

"In *Disciplined Dreaming*, Josh Linkner offers a guide for encouraging and protecting creativity as one of the few sustainable advantages in a relentlessly competitive environment. I would recommend it highly for the leaders and advisors to any high-growth organization."

—**Victor E. Parker,** managing director, Spectrum Equity Investors

DISCIPLINED DREAMING

A PROVEN SYSTEM TO DRIVE BREAKTHROUGH CREATIVITY

Josh Linkner

JOSSEY-BASS
A Wiley Imprint
www.josseybass.com

Copyright © 2011 by Josh Linkner. All rights reserved.

Published by Jossey-Bass
A Wiley Imprint
989 Market Street, San Francisco, CA 94103-1741—www.josseybass.com

No part of this publication may be reproduced, stored in a retrieval system, or transmitted in any form or by any means, electronic, mechanical, photocopying, recording, scanning, or otherwise, except as permitted under Section 107 or 108 of the 1976 United States Copyright Act, without either the prior written permission of the publisher, or authorization through payment of the appropriate per-copy fee to the Copyright Clearance Center, Inc., 222 Rosewood Drive, Danvers, MA 01923, 978-750-8400, fax 978-646-8600, or on the Web at www.copyright.com. Requests to the publisher for permission should be addressed to the Permissions Department, John Wiley & Sons, Inc., 111 River Street, Hoboken, NJ 07030, 201-748-6011, fax 201-748-6008, or online at www.wiley.com/go/permissions.

Readers should be aware that Internet Web sites offered as citations and/or sources for further information may have changed or disappeared between the time this was written and when it is read.

Limit of Liability/Disclaimer of Warranty: While the publisher and author have used their best efforts in preparing this book, they make no representations or warranties with respect to the accuracy or completeness of the contents of this book and specifically disclaim any implied warranties of merchantability or fitness for a particular purpose. No warranty may be created or extended by sales representatives or written sales materials. The advice and strategies contained herein may not be suitable for your situation. You should consult with a professional where appropriate. Neither the publisher nor author shall be liable for any loss of profit or any other commercial damages, including but not limited to special, incidental, consequential, or other damages.

Jossey-Bass books and products are available through most bookstores. To contact Jossey-Bass directly call our Customer Care Department within the U.S. at 800-956-7739, outside the U.S. at 317-572-3986, or fax 317-572-4002.

Jossey-Bass also publishes its books in a variety of electronic formats. Some content that appears in print may not be available in electronic books.

Library of Congress Cataloging-in-Publication Data
Linkner, Josh, 1970-
   Disciplined dreaming : a proven system to drive breakthrough creativity / Josh Linkner.
      p. cm.
   Includes bibliographical references and index.
   ISBN 978-0-470-92222-4 (cloth); ISBN 978-1-118-00169-1 (ebk); ISBN 978-1-118-00170-7 (ebk); ISBN 978-1-118-00171-4 (ebk)
   1. Creative ability in business. 2. Success in business. I. Title.
   HD53.L56 2011
   650.1—dc22

                                                                        2010046965

Printed in the United States of America

FIRST EDITION

HB Printing 10 9 8 7 6 5 4 3 2

To my incredibly creative kids,
Noah and Chloe

Contents

STEP FOUR Ignite

STEP FIVE Launch

Preface

I've had the good fortune to straddle the art world and the business world for the last twenty years. I started performing traditional jazz guitar professionally at the age of thirteen. I would sneak into bars in Detroit, and often played until either the gig ended or I got thrown out. After graduating high school, I attended the Berklee School of Music, then went on to perform internationally, teach lessons, compose music, and study with some of the best musicians in the world. I still perform today, with the GEQ Quintet—a high-intensity, traditional jazz group.

Perhaps surprisingly, jazz has been an outstanding training ground for me as an entrepreneur and business leader. The skills I learned playing jazz translate perfectly into the business world: improvising, dealing with adversity, working through uncertainty, blending collaboration with individual performance, and, most important, creating value through original thought and imagination.

I have launched four high-tech businesses, the most recent being ePrize, which I founded in 1999. At that time, Internet advertising was the darling of the high-flying dot-com world. There were hundreds of emerging online advertising companies. As a marketer, I found it odd that an entire category of the marketing mix—promotions—was largely ignored online. And there was my golden ticket—an opportunity to zag when everyone was zigging, to do the never-been-done-before. ePrize went on to rewrite the rules of a one-hundred-year-old industry.

Within our first five years, we became the dominant player in the world of online promotion, developing more games, contests, and sweepstakes than any other company in the world, both online and offline. The company grew to 350 people with offices in New York, Detroit, Chicago, Dallas, Los Angeles, Atlanta, and London. We gained experience running promotions in thirty-seven countries for seventy-four of the top one hundred brands, including Coca-Cola, American Express, Disney, General Mills, P&G, the Gap, Nike, and Microsoft. In ePrize's ninth full year of business, its gross sales exceeded $70 million.

In the midst of this success, I grew curious. An honest look in the mirror revealed an okay technology guy, an average finance person (at best), and a so-so organizational leader. The more I explored, the more I realized that there was one primary differentiator that fueled my success and allowed me to break the mold: creativity.

I also realized how creatively bankrupt most companies are today. With a constant focus on cost cutting, efficiency gains, and top-down control, too many organizations have lost their mojo. The problem is exacerbated by the ever-escalating arms race for competitive edge. When the dust settles, the only thing that can't be commoditized is creativity. Creativity is what will separate the winners from the also-rans in the emerging world of business—and in life.

That epiphany launched me into a whole new gig. I became obsessed with demystifying creativity and developing a specific system that could be used to nurture, manage, and grow creative capacity. In the process, I interviewed more than two hundred thought leaders, including CEOs, billionaires, musicians, entrepreneurs, artists, educators, and nonprofit leaders, to examine how they used creativity to drive their own success. This book and the Disciplined Dreaming system it describes are the result of that journey, my own riff on exploring and exploiting the vital link that joins creativity and success in business. I hope you enjoy it.

December 2010   Josh Linkner
Detroit, Michigan

DISCIPLINED DREAMING

Introduction

Only four measures are left before it's my turn to solo, and the adrenaline rush is overwhelming. The dimly lit, smoky jazz club is packed with local aficionados. Guymon Ensley, the bandleader, finishes his scorching trumpet solo, and the crowd erupts with applause. The attention turns to me, as it's now my turn to improvise.

With less than 1 percent of the notes on the written page, I have to make up the rest as I go—spontaneous creativity in real time, no going back to correct mistakes or rethink a passage. The pressure is on, but then again so is the excitement. It's time to bring everything I have to this moment, to deliver a sound that's both technically pure and infused with creativity. Passion and skill must work together to form something new, a jazz performance that works with the other pros around me, that is true to me as a musician, and that satisfies the hypercritical and quite knowledgeable audience.

Replace the musical references here with business lingo, and this scenario describes the daily life of thousands of businesspeople across industries. Like jazz, business success is most often based on creativity and original thought, not technical mastery. Jazz and business legends—people like John Coltrane and Billie Holiday or Henry Ford and Bill Gates—are remembered because of what they created.

Imagine a computer playing a jazz solo; the music would be technically proficient, but lacking in emotion and original thought. That's the same kind of "music" being played by countless businesses today. As economies and world markets continue to change, businesses are constantly being pulled into cost cutting, automation, and risk management. Although these are important elements of business success, we can't lose sight of the driving force of prosperity, the reason that any company exists in the first place, the source of both business and human fulfillment: *creativity*.

Why You Need to Care About Creativity

Nearly all of the more than two hundred people I interviewed in my research for this book credited creativity as a critically important factor in the success of their company and career. I expected to hear this from artists, musicians, and marketing folks. But I was surprised and delighted to hear the same from finance executives, hard-nosed CEOs, nonprofit leaders, bankers, and even military leaders. Universally, this amazing group of thought leaders stated that creativity was one of the most important ingredients of their success, if not the most important.

Scott Dorsey, the founder and CEO of Exact Target, credits creativity for his success in growing a market-leading $100 million e-mail marketing business with five hundred employees in less than a decade. "Our willingness to embrace creative problem solving and experimentation enabled our growth at every level—from raising capital to developing technology to winning customers. Creativity was the key ingredient."[1]

Steven Bean, CEO of Universal Laundry, feels the same way. "Creativity is fundamentally responsible for the success and direction of both my company and my career. It impacts our strategy, marketing, and business processes."[2]

John Balardo, publisher of Hour Media, agrees on the impact creativity has had on his career. "Creativity has been paramount in my success. The highest level of importance. We are in a highly competitive industry that is becoming increasing commoditized. It is a cluttered industry, with tough competitors fighting ruthlessly for share of mind. In our case, we must offer something different and compelling. That's where creativity comes in. Without it, we wouldn't stand a chance. This is especially true in tough times. When things get rough, we need to double down on our creative efforts in order to stand out."[3]

An overwhelming majority of those I interviewed also told me of their concern about an increasing dearth of creativity in the business world. They are worried that they lack specific systems to build, nurture, and manage creativity and are concerned that they could begin to lose competitive advantage unless this trend is reversed. When rating the importance of creativity in the business world, the group averaged 8.9 on a scale from 1 to 10 (10 being the highest). But how did they rate their organizations in terms of being prepared to meet that creative demand? The ratings averaged only 4.7.

These dismal numbers confirm what many business leaders already know: we have an increasing need for creativity in the business world, but a decreasing supply—conflicting trends that have created a large and growing creativity gap. For perhaps the first time in our history, American creativity is on the decline. In fact, researcher Kyung Hee Kim at the College of William and Mary has found that predictors of creativity among our population rose steadily until 1990, but have been inching downward ever since, in what Kim describes as a "very significant decrease."[4]

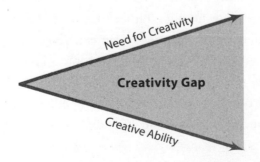

The creativity gap will determine the economic potential of every individual and organization in the years ahead. You have to address this gap in your own life and organization if you plan to grow your career, if your company plans on winning in the future, and if our country is to maintain its standing in the world as an economic superpower. Closing the creativity gap is what *Disciplined Dreaming* is all about.

What to Expect from *Disciplined Dreaming*

Disciplined Dreaming is a system for expanding creative capacity, fueling competitive advantage, and building personal and professional growth. This book describes that system and offers a proven framework for generating creativity. Businesses have systems and processes for everything, from answering the phone to taking out the trash. Remarkably, most companies have no such system for the one thing that matters most: developing and growing creative capacity. Disciplined Dreaming provides a specific system to attack any Creativity Challenge, big or small, and, in the process, to build a culture of creativity and sustained growth for individuals and their organizations.

Companies that have "innovation processes" often stifle the creativity of their organization by making those processes too rule driven, formal, and restrictive. In contrast, Disciplined Dreaming is an open system that focuses on the creative mind-set and philosophy along with specific techniques, rather than a rigid code of rules. I've based this system on my own ideas and experiences, as well as those of successful business leaders around the globe. This book is a guide to that system, not an instruction manual.

The first two chapters outline the compelling case for creativity in building business success and introduce you to the Disciplined

Dreaming system for creative growth. The remaining sections of this book follow the five-step methodology of Disciplined Dreaming:

Step 1: Ask. The first step of the Disciplined Dreaming process is identifying and clearly defining your specific Creativity Challenge (whatever its size). In Chapters Three and Four, you'll learn how to define your Creativity Challenge while driving curiosity and awareness in order to focus the energy of your team.

Step 2: Prepare. Next, you have to make sure you're ready to meet the challenge you've identified. Chapters Five and Six offer key concepts for preparing yourself mentally and physically for the creative process and for positioning your environment for maximum creative output.

Step 3: Discover. In the Discover phase of Disciplined Dreaming, you explore every avenue that might lead to creative ideas. Chapter Seven offers a wealth of techniques for charting your creative road map.

Step 4: Ignite. Now you're ready to let your imagination soar. Chapters Eight and Nine outline proven techniques for sparking creativity and generating more (and better) creative ideas.

Step 5: Launch. Your final step is to make your best creative ideas a reality. Chapter Ten outlines a framework for selecting your best ideas and putting them into action.

As you read, you will find a step-by-step process with stories, examples, and practical exercises that you can put to use immediately in order to become more effective and to develop your creative chops. The book offers plenty of inspiration, but it also provides specific and practical takeaways to drive the success of your company and your career. You'll find plenty of frontline insights from the interviews I've conducted, along with my own observations and experiences. Improvisation is a spontaneous burst of creativity, and to keep the tempo brisk, this book gives a nod to many of the strong and sometimes surprising links between improvisational jazz and business innovation.

Disciplined Dreaming is a methodology that can help anyone—from the single mom raising her kids to the freshly graduated engineer growing her career; from the clinical psychologist working to connect with his patients to the local deli owner looking to bring more hungry customers in the door at lunchtime on Tuesdays—find more creative solutions to the challenges he or she faces. Although many of us have let our creativity fade over the years, each of us has an abundance of creativity within. This book will give you a system for revealing your unique creative nature. Get ready to let your ideas come out and play.

1

•

The Case for Creativity

If you don't like change, you're going to like irrelevance even less.
—GENERAL ERICK SHINSEKI

A friend recently came to me to ask for advice about his business, a promotional products company. He lamented that he was stuck: revenue was flat, and he couldn't seem to get to the next level. I began to toss out ideas of new ways to get customers, approach the market, expand his offerings, and improve his processes. With each suggestion, his reply was, "No. That's not the way it's done in my industry."

After a few rounds of this, I decided to give him some straight-between-the-eyes feedback: "If you're unwilling to be different," I said, "you'll *never* get to the next level. The very fact that the entire industry does something a particular way is a great reason to explore the exact opposite approach."

My friend isn't alone in the challenges he faces. In this post-recession era, just about every industry is in the midst of massive upheaval, with companies hyperfocused on cost cutting, efficiency gains, and "sticking to their knitting." You can only cut so far, though, and at some point you need to innovate and grow in order to win. The business world is at a critical inflection point, leaving companies with that dreaded choice: adapt or die—which makes this the perfect time for you to focus on finding new and more creative ways to beat your competitors.

The Risky Business of Playing It Safe

In this new democratized world, competitive advantage has a short shelf life. We've entered the Age of Creativity, in which each incremental gain is zeroed out as global competitors quickly copy and adapt. There are four factors fueling the creativity arms race:

1. *Commoditization.* In the words of casino magnate Steve Wynn, "What used to draw a 'wow' 15 years ago wouldn't draw a yawn today."[1] Easily accessible and free online information makes new knowledge a readily available commodity, which can leave price as the sole differentiating factor among competitors. You can't grow a career or business strictly by being the lowest bidder.

2. *Speed.* Complete business cycles that used to span a decade or more now play out in a matter of months. It's no longer about the big beating the small. Now it is the fast beating the slow.

3. *Low barriers.* In the past, bringing a great idea to market might require significant resources—a huge outlay of capital, a factory, raw materials, labor contracts, and distribution. Those barriers made competitors fewer in number and easier to identify. Today, a kid in his college dorm room with a high-speed Internet connection launches Facebook and becomes a billionaire in twenty-four months.

4. *Lower costs.* Globalization, outsourcing, and an intense cost-cutting mentality in the business world have driven costs to their lowest levels in history. The price war has now become just one skirmish on a much more complex battleground.

The world doesn't need another "me-too" player. Consumers have nearly limitless choices of products and services. Employees now compete with others around the globe for jobs. Strong technical skills, quality, and good service once won the game, but today they're just the ante. Success in the new era of business is driven by your ability to stand out and be truly remarkable. That requires an ability to tap into creativity, break the mold, introduce disruptive change, and dislodge the status quo.

Over my career, I've been in the fortunate position of being the dislodging force rather than the one being dislodged. I've also seen that the top of the heap is no place to relax and think "If it ain't broke, don't fix it."

In the sweepstakes world, one company in New York dominated the industry for twenty-five years—then it didn't. Think how it must have stung when ePrize, a small upstart company from Detroit, came along and took the lead with 83 percent more programs. Or how sharp the pain was the next year when our lead rose to 260 percent.

Like all change agents and creative disrupters, we didn't win because we executed the old model more efficiently. Change agents win because they have the courage and creativity to break the mold. Red Bull broke the mold by launching an entirely new beverage category: the energy drink. Michael Dell broke the mold by selling computers directly to the consumer and cutting out the middleman. Jazz legend Charlie Parker broke the mold by challenging conventional wisdom and playing previously "forbidden" notes over smoking fast-tempo chord changes.

Great companies are always built on ideas. They discover new and compelling ways to solve problems for customers. They play to win rather than playing not-to-lose. In fact, we've reached a time when playing it safe has become the riskiest move of all. General

Motors played it safe all the way to bankruptcy. Maxwell House played it safe as the more daring and creative Starbucks supplanted it as leader of the coffee industry.

This concept applies not only to breakthrough corporate innovation but also to individual careers. Have you ever looked at the Forbes 400 list of the wealthiest Americans? To qualify these days, you need to be *at least* a billionaire—pretty high stakes. In reviewing the list, I noticed something right away: there are no Forbes 400 billionaires who earned their wealth by playing it safe, cutting costs, and following the rules. Quite the opposite: every one of these people did something new and different. From retail to software to manufacturing to creating a new kind of candy bar, the ideas these people generated changed the world. And in every case, the genesis of their success traces back to a lightning bolt of creative inspiration.

Why aren't more of us channeling that creative energy? Blame it on the gremlin—that invisible source of self-doubt that sits on our shoulder and reminds us of every negative adult, teacher, boss, coworker, media analyst, or other influence that discouraged us from embracing those bolts of inspiration. The gremlin holds us back. He fills us with fear and tells us to keep our thoughts to ourselves. He makes us believe that letting our creativity out will make us look foolish or doom us to failure. This gremlin is, of course, dead wrong. The people in companies that thrive ignore their gremlins.

At the end of the day, ***the only sustainable competitive advantage—for individuals and companies—is creativity***. It can't be copied or replicated. It can't be outsourced to the lowest bidder. It can't be done faster overseas. Creativity will build our future, just as it's built our past. As we have done throughout history, we ignore those who huddle in fear, and celebrate and reward the risk-takers, innovators, and creators.

How Will Creativity Rewrite Your Future?

You may be thinking, "Well, that's great, but I'm not a billionaire. I don't want to start and build my own company. I'm not an inventor. All this doesn't really apply to me." That's your gremlin talking, and he's wrong—again.

The concept of leveraging creativity to grow success applies regardless of who you are, what your job currently is, or where you're positioned on an organization chart. People who demonstrate curiosity and courage become indispensable to their companies. They get promoted and rewarded. People who can imagine new alternatives to tough problems help nonprofit organizations increase impact. People who explore boundaries and try new approaches in education are the ones who make a difference—the ones schoolkids remember.

What is happening in your industry? Can you truly afford to sit back and rely on your past success? How are you going to win on the next leg of your journey? Will you be the disruptive force of change through courageous risk-taking and breathtaking creativity, or will you be like so many people, shrugging your shoulders wondering what happened to your business? Let's look at just three ways that creativity will determine the answers to these questions.

Succeeding Through Improvisation and Risk-Taking

Business culture is beginning to reward improvisational "players" who, like great jazz musicians, are comfortable taking risks and capable of extraordinary and spontaneous bursts of creativity. Jazz musicians are a curious breed. They study for years to master the rules, only to break them as quickly as possible. They approach their craft with intensity and purpose, but then can let go and just groove when the feeling is right. I've known musicians who are incredibly bold and expressive on the bandstand, but thoughtful and tempered in conversation.

All these dissonant notes blend into the creative harmony of a culture that encourages risk-taking and shuns sameness. Jazz combos don't just accept the improvisation and risk-taking that goes along with creativity; their entire purpose is to be creative. Oddly, most businesses don't connect their purpose with creativity. They have mission statements packed with industry buzzwords, but most of them are completely missing the point of their organization's existence: to create new and better ideas.

How APRIL Links Business and Jazz

Jazz musician and author Michael Gold agrees that the same principles that make jazz groups succeed also drive successful businesses. He's collected these principles under the acronym APRIL:[2]

Autonomy. Team members are in control of their own performance, experience, and results.

Passion. "Players" are driven by something bigger than just the task at hand.

Risk. The working environment celebrates risk and failure.

Innovation. New ideas are rewarded.

Listening. The culture emphasizes raising awareness and connecting to the environment.

How does your organization stack up against the APRIL principles? Do you encourage autonomy or seek control? Is passion a buzzword, or do you demonstrate and reward it? Is *risk* a taboo four-letter word? Is innovation "owned" only by those at the top, or is forging new ground an assignment for everyone at all levels of the organization? How do you communicate with your colleagues, suppliers, and customers?

As I grew ePrize from an idea into the dominant industry leader, improvisation—creating something out of nothing, in real time—was as central to my business as it is to jazz. The business had the frenetic energy of a live jazz gig, often a little off balance, but always exhilarating. We didn't have an instruction manual; we had to make things up as we went along. Some decisions failed; some worked out. Either way, we kept things fast, fluid, and creative. We were decisive even in the face of ambiguity. And when we made mistakes, we learned from them quickly and adapted.

We were fluid with our offerings. We listened to what the client wanted, and if we thought that we could improve and build it for them, we'd take the job. This improvisational mind-set fueled our R&D efforts. Many of our best, most sustainable products originally came from a one-off client request. The client would request a new type of promotion, and we would work around the clock to develop the product as though we already had it. Rather than building a bunch of products in the hope that they would sell some day, we would wait until we had a buyer and then use the revenue from that client to fund our product development. We bit off more than we could chew, and then chewed as fast as we could. Real-time R&D, jazz style.

Companies that will win in the future will function more like jazz bands. They will constantly reinvent their work and seek fresh, new approaches. They will reward risk-taking and originality, the new currency for success. And although businesses will always have leaders, as organizational structures flatten, everyone's voice will have a greater chance of being heard. Your ability to improvise and your comfort with risk-taking will determine how well you succeed in this increasingly creative culture.

Thriving in an Adapt-or-Die Marketplace

People fear change. When a radical new idea emerges, it is almost always met with criticism, resistance, and doubt. Even though clinging tightly to the status quo feels safe, it's one of riskiest moves you can make. In an adapt-or-die marketplace, creativity is the air supply that keeps individuals and organizations thriving.

> *Out there is an entrepreneur who is forging a bullet with your company's name on it. You've got one option now—to shoot first. You've got to out-innovate the innovators.*
>
> —GARY HAMEL

When I launched ePrize, I had plenty of naysayers telling me my ideas would never work. But that rain of negativity only fueled my determination to succeed. I set out to build a company that would essentially reinvent itself on a continuous basis. My favorite saying was (and is), "Someday, a company is going to come along and put us out of business. It might as well be us." In 1999, when I told the first employee I hired that he wouldn't recognize ePrize in six months, I had no idea how right I was.

Within months, the dot-com meltdown had turned the once-fashionable "e" at the front of an organization's name into a scarlet letter. The small, venture-backed companies that made up our customer base were dropping like flies. My young company faced a huge challenge: adapt or die.

The solution was pretty simple: we needed to stop focusing on the Petfood.coms of the world and turn our attention to the P&Gs. We had to adapt all our technology, product, and service offerings to fit the needs of large-brand clients—which required a lot of creativity and a willingness to completely upend industry norms. We kicked around endless ideas, until we finally came up with three winning strategies:

1. *Relentless selling*. At that time, many marketing and promotion agencies waited for their phones to ring and prided themselves on never having to "sell." I took the opposite approach. I hired

the best people I could find and then trained them to be a killer sales force. We conducted role-playing drills. We made target lists and pursued them with vigor. We used a go-to-market strategy of aggressive, direct selling in a world that never had seen such a thing.

2. *Building the brand*. We realized that our brand had to look bigger than the size of our company. Our sales materials were beautifully designed and printed on the best paper. An aggressive PR effort got us featured in trade journals and business publications to establish third-party credibility. We positioned ourselves as the expert and leader in a new category within our industry—digital promotions.

3. *Offering something unique*. We worked hard to develop a few products and features that no one else was offering. Potential clients wanted to meet with us just so they could learn about the "next new thing." That gave us an opening and often got us an initial order.

Our organization's creative muscle helped us thrive in the changing marketplace, while our less creative competitors failed to adapt—and then died. Today, variations on this same song of survival are playing out in organizations around the world, and in every case, creativity is the one constant note.

People and organizations turn their backs on change out of fear, allowing bureaucratic cogs in the machine to get in the way of great ideas and dreams. Twenty years from now, they'll be long gone, and organizations who walk boldly and create something new will dominate the marketplace. The risks you take in leveraging creative ideas are much less than those you take when sitting in stunned silence as opportunity passes you by. More than an essential survival skill, creativity is the key to thriving in a rapidly evolving marketplace.

Focusing Bets on the Future

All companies make decisions about where to place their bets. We're all faced with limited resources (time, money, talent) and have to choose where to deploy those resources in order to reach our goals. Although most companies begin with a bolt of creative inspiration, it takes real creative capacity to make the choices that will keep an organization energized and growing into the future.

As a company matures, its focus can slowly shift from creativity to execution. Real customers and employees and vendors demand attention, leaving less time in the day to ponder the universe and think up cool new ideas. As leaders focus on building systems and processes to run the place, a bureaucracy is born. Territories form and creativity drops, as the company bets all its resources on protecting the golden goose that established its place in the industry. In the past, this model could sustain a business for years or even decades, but in the new world of business, it just doesn't fly.

Microsoft is a great example of the dangers of betting on the past instead of the future. Windows and Office remain dominant in the market, and have generated over $100 billion in profit for Microsoft in the last ten years alone.[3] For years, Microsoft was the poster child of innovation and thought leadership; but then its focus began shifting to past successes, causing the company to miss out on important advances. While Microsoft placed its bets on an established customer adaptation cycle, its competitors innovated. So the company lost to Kindle, Sony, and Apple in the e-book world. It lost to Google in the Internet search world. It lost to Wikipedia in the online encyclopedia market, and it lost to Apple iPod in the digital music sphere. And Microsoft completely missed mobile phones and tablet PCs.

The rate of change in the new era of business has dramatically accelerated, and ever-shorter product life cycles put ever-greater demands on creative capacity. The new model for winning a better future is to remain on the forefront of innovation. To do that, organizations have to use their resources to place smarter bets, earlier and faster. That requires the creative foresight to know when it's time to shift investments forward—even if it means sacrificing the golden goose.

Are You Ready to Become a Disruptive Force of Change?

You may not like it, you may wish things were different, you may look fondly at the past, but none of this matters: the rules have changed. The financial meltdown and global recession of 2009, combined with globalization, rapid advances in technology and communications, population trends, geopolitical movements, and a next-generation workforce, have made the past irrelevant. These changes punctuate the end of an era and signify the beginning of a new one.

> *All truth passes through three stages. First, it is ridiculed. Second, it is violently opposed. Third, it is accepted as self-evident.*
>
> —ARTHUR SCHOPENHAUER

This revolution isn't about just digital promotions or eBook readers or online shoe stores. Nearly every industry is in the midst of transformation. Careers and jobs are being dislodged and reinvented at a dizzying pace. For you and your company to win in the Age of Creativity, you need to nurture and develop your creative skills, to become more like an artist than a technician. In this marketplace, you have to be able to add value in the face of uncertainty. You can't rely on a rule book to figure out what to do next. Instead, your rewards will be based on fresh ideas, improvisation, and a willingness to release your grip on the status quo. You need to be the disruptive force of change, or you run the risk of getting knocked out of the competition.

Building Your Creativity Chops

Jazz musicians call the time and effort they invest in developing their musical skill "building chops." The Disciplined Dreaming system I'll introduce to you in the next chapter of this book brings you a framework of ideas, processes, and practices for building *your* chops by expanding your creative capacity. At the close of most chapters of this book, you'll find a short list of ideas and activities aimed at helping you assess and review what you've learned, like a jazz artist practicing musical scales. In this first set, you can answer the following questions to gain a clearer picture of the way you currently approach the creative process:

1. What percentage of your time is spent creating something new, as opposed to working out operational details or protecting the past?
2. List five ways that you can beat your competition. How could they beat you?
3. If you were entering your industry as a start-up, how would you break the mold to beat the incumbents?
4. What elements of the past or status quo are you clinging to? What do you need to let go of?
5. How could placing your bets earlier drive your bottom line?
6. List five ways your company is stagnating; for each of these, list at least two ideas addressing how you can break through those barriers.

2

Disciplined Dreaming

Your System for Creativity

There is nothing more difficult to plan, more doubtful of success, more dangerous to manage than the creation of a new system.

—MACHIAVELLI

Charlie Parker was a groundbreaking jazz musician of the 1940s. He was a creative genius, a pioneer, a legend. In his day, Parker was so influential in the jazz community that people went to great lengths to emulate his brilliance, even his heroin habit. Nearly seventy years later, his influence is still felt in every jazz club in the world.

Parker's impact had nothing to do with his compositions; his written music was average at best. He wasn't known for being a great side-man and playing exactly what others put on the page. In fact, he was erratic and difficult to work with. What Parker was known for was his amazing ability to improvise—his brilliant spontaneous creativity.

But even Charlie Parker, one of the most creative people to ever live, used a *structure* to release his creativity. Although most of what you hear in a jazz performance is improvised, there is still an important underlying framework that allows the musicians to weave their musical lines and express their emotions. In music terms, this structure includes key signature, tempo, time signature, chord progression, section layout, and general style (swing, bop, ballad, blues, and so on). It also can include some other guideposts, such as how to treat the intro or ending of a song or how to deal with the solo section.

You might think that any framework or guideline restricts creativity, but in fact, it does just the opposite. The structure in jazz *enables* creativity. It forms the system of notes, chords, styles, layouts, and other elements that provide boundaries to explore and a common framework for collaboration. The chords guide the musicians as they choose notes to sound mellow or harsh, to build tension in their listeners or ease them into relaxation. The style allows the group to connect with influences of the past while still forging new ground. The structure helps the group produce a unified sound.

Jazz without structure, called free jazz, sounds dissonant and disjointed to most listeners; it's a collection of random instrument noises with little creative glue to unify the sound. In fact, creativity needs some type of structure or system to give it form and to encourage its development.

Structure enables your creativity, too. If I asked you to come up with a metaphor for your business, you could find it a daunting task. But if I provided some additional structure by, say, asking you to tell me why your business is like a pencil, the job becomes much easier. You might tell me that to reach your full potential you need to stay sharp, or that you're always willing to accept risk because you can correct mistakes. If I asked you to come up with an idea for a new product, my request might be too vague to spark any ideas. In contrast, if the assignment was to produce ideas for a personal care product using Greek mythology as a metaphor, you might come up with Medusa Moistening Shampoo or Aphrodite Aromatherapy or Zeus Shaving Cream—for the Strongest of Men. Like a member of a jazz combo, you are freed to be creative within a specific structure.

What most businesses and individuals lack isn't raw creative talent. What they lack is a system to unleash it. Even organizations who have systems for nearly every aspect of their business, from answering the phone to setting the security alarm, have no system for developing and managing creativity. The most important thing a company can do is thus left to happen by chance. Managers take creativity for granted, yet wonder why they are not achieving growth and success. I developed the Disciplined Dreaming system to give creativity its own place and practice, to provide everyone in the organization a structure for developing his or her own creative ideas, and to bring creativity back to the heart of business—where it belongs.

Disciplined Dreaming at a Glance

The Disciplined Dreaming framework will enable you to develop and grow your own creative capacity and that of your team. It has specific frameworks and techniques to guide you through each phase of the creative process and to help you connect with your own artistic abilities.

In developing the Disciplined Dreaming methodology, I examined where, in my experience as an entrepreneur and musician, I had made mistakes, and how I had developed ideas that propelled me to the cutting edge of the marketing, technology, and business worlds. I examined the successes of the most innovative brands on the planet, and I asked questions of other leaders who had leveraged their creative capabilities to redefine their industries. How did they do it? What techniques did they use to spark creativity or to restrict it?

I used the results to develop a system for creativity that anyone can use to build his or her own creative chops. The system balances the need for structure with the equally important requirement of allowing freedom of expression. The five steps of the Disciplined Dreaming process provide adequate scaffolding, without imposing rigid limits that could kill creative fire. Let's take a closer look at them.

Step 1: Ask

You begin the Disciplined Dreaming process by setting clearly defined objectives for finding a creative solution to a specific problem—your Creativity Challenge. Defining your target through the use of a Creativity Brief allows you to fully articulate the situation at hand, so you can direct raw creativity (yours and your team's) in a purposeful way. The Ask phase is all about asking questions, exploring possibilities, and awakening curiosity and awareness.

Step 2: Prepare

In the same way that athletes and musicians warm up in order to give their best performance, you benefit greatly by preparing to be creative. In this step, you set the stage for the Disciplined Dreaming process by preparing every aspect of your mind, body, and environment to support maximum creative performance. You'll warm up your mind-set and emotional state by clearing away the hurdles of some common myths and pitfalls that can block the creative process. You'll prepare your physical environment to provide an atmosphere that's fun, surprising, and a fertile garden for growing creativity. And you will take specific steps to ensure that your culture is optimized to nurture creativity and to get out of the way and let it flow.

Step 3: Discover

You were born with an abundance of creativity, and it's still there within you. The Discover phase gives you the treasure map to uncover creative ideas and bring them to the surface. In this step, you'll use concepts like the Borrowed Idea, inflection points, the Upside Down, and patterns to get in touch with your creative nature and to jump-start your imagination.

Step 4: Ignite

With the foundation in place from steps 1 through 3, you are now ready to let your ideas fly free. You will begin by generating creative sparks with techniques including Imbizo groups, the Hot Potato, and the Wrong Answer. You will then develop those sparks into fully formed ideas with eight powerful idea generation techniques, including EdgeStorming, the Long List, RoleStorming, and Brain Writing.

Step 5: Launch

In the final phase of Disciplined Dreaming, your analytical side is reconnected with your creativity, as whole-brain thinking goes to work. The tasks you perform in this phase put your creative ideas into action, as you select your best ideas, determine key metrics for measurement, and build an action plan to bring your ideas to life.

■ ■ ■

The Disciplined Dreaming methodology may feel a bit formal at first, but will become much more fluid with practice. As it does when learning to play an instrument, mastery requires time and practice—and the Disciplined Dreaming system also provides a set of creativity exercises that can guide you in that practice. I recommend that you get comfortable with the system by tackling smaller Creativity Challenges first, then build toward giant innovation projects. Each person (and team) can move through the experience at his or her own pace, based on his or her background, industry, and current level of creative expression. As I've said before, Disciplined Dreaming is an open system that focuses on developing a mind-set, philosophy, and practice for finding new, creative, and innovative ideas. It's not a set of strict rules for arriving at a bland and uninspired take on the same old thing.

Getting the Most from Disciplined Dreaming

We've already seen some of the baseline benefits you can expect to achieve by using the Disciplined Dreaming system. You've seen that you can use the system to get unstuck by breaking free from artificial barriers to creativity. Disciplined Dreaming can also help you tap into the hidden brainpower inside you and your company, and establish an ongoing system to nurture and harvest your team's best ideas. By using the system, you'll also

- Avoid costly mistakes of flawed ideas and measurement
- Increase your ability to deal with ambiguity and uncertainty
- Learn how to adapt more quickly and proactively to changes in the marketplace
- Apply focused creativity to specific business problems of all shapes and sizes

Let's take a closer look at how you can apply Disciplined Dreaming to achieve these benefits.

Exploding Limited Definitions of Creativity

Part of the problem we have in engaging our creative energy comes from our sometimes limited view of what actually "qualifies" as creativity. Some consider creativity to be an artistic pursuit, more useful in the artist's studio than the conference room. Others think of creativity in terms of tasks or professions—chefs are creative, accountants aren't. To get the most from the Disciplined Dreaming system, you need to abandon such limited notions and embrace a broader and more expansive concept of creativity.

When I asked thought leaders in personal interviews how they defined creativity, nearly every one had a broad, no-limits take on the term. Here are some of my favorites:

- "The ability to build something from nothing"—Ted Murphy, founder and CEO, Izea.com
- "The ability to think of a common idea in an uncommon way"—Randall Dunn, head of the Roeper School
- "The ability to take a concept, task, idea, or product and enlarge it . . . to move it to new directions never contemplated"—Bernie Bergman, CEO, Bare Essentials
- "More of a feeling of inspiration. Being audacious, wild. Allowing yourself to be vulnerable and giving yourself freedom to be inspired."—Jeff Bennett, founder and CEO, OtterBase
- "A passion to do something different. To be original. To build, to invent, to make."—Brian Gillespie, creative director, BarComm
- "Problem solving. You can be creative in how you polish your shoes. It is the approach you take."—Ernie Perich, founder and CEO, Perich + Partners
- "The proactive ability to think through, weigh, and judge alternatives to problem solving. Seeing multiple ways of viewing things."—Lisa Vallee-Smith, founder and CEO, Airfoil Public Relations
- "Connecting things that aren't connected. The ability to think differently. To be able to turn the ship and manage through uncertainty."—Jake Sigal, founder and CEO, Myine Electronics
- "There are two aspects: (1) to create something from nothing; (2) the ability to adapt to a given situation. To take what you

are given and make it better or different."—Jeff Ponders, jazz musician

- "The basis is curiosity. Structuring unstructured things. The ability to tolerate ambiguity and create something new that is not patently obvious."—Steven Bean, CEO, Universal Laundry Systems
- "Bringing something into existence from nothing. Finding nonobvious answers that add new value."—Amjad Hussain, founder and CEO, Silk Route Global

A limited notion of creativity limits your ability to create. "The truth is that all sorts of people, possessing various levels of natural ability, are capable of engaging in fulfilling creative processes," according to Carlin Flora, the features editor at *Psychology Today*. "Buying into a limited definition of creativity prevents many from appreciating their own potential."[1]

Like a musician exploring a totally new take on a jazz standard, you will use the structure of the Disciplined Dreaming framework to reshape your approach to creativity, rather than trying to mold the process to fit your preconceived notions of who can, or should, be creative or where creativity is necessary or "appropriate." Let the system lead you toward a new and expanded understanding of creativity and its role in your personal and professional life.

Developing Your Creativity DNA

Although every business offers infinite possibilities for creative expression, most Creativity Challenges require solutions that fall into one of three categories:

1. *Breakthrough Innovation.* Creativity Challenges in this category call for game-changing innovations that rewrite the rules of the

game. Examples include the assembly line, the iPod, Google, the electric guitar, and Swiffer. Breakthrough Innovations are the legends that people read about in magazines and study in business schools.

2. *High-Value Change.* The solutions to this type of Creativity Challenge result in significant improvements in product offerings, processes, or business approaches that drive tangible value. Examples include a new product add-on that delights customers and increases sales by 14 percent, a new production process that improves efficiency by 23 percent, or a new marketing campaign that drives an immediate 11 percent boost in revenue.

3. *Everyday Creativity.* These are the creative solutions that change the way you and your company think and behave in everyday work—small changes in high frequency that add up to big results. Examples include better results on a customer service call, more productive and fulfilling weekly staff meetings, or better close rates for sales reps.

Disciplined Dreaming helps you boost your capabilities in all three of these categories of creativity, and that's important for your overall creative growth. Breakthrough Innovation and High-Value Change are the acceleration points that propel you over your competitors and to the leading edge of your industry. But you'll begin by focusing the Disciplined Dreaming system on building your Everyday Creativity, because that's the fuel that keeps you and your organization performing at maximum capability.

Everyday Creativity is a concept that is critical to organizational success in today's ultracompetitive world. Simply put, it means exhibiting creativity on a continuous basis, at every level of the org chart. Everyday Creativity is one salesperson winning the deal over another by using a fresh, creative approach to solving the customer's needs. It appears when a customer service representative engenders loyalty instead of indifference. It's the small improvements made by a software engineer that end up saving her company millions of dollars through increased productivity, or the argument that a trial lawyer uses to win a jury verdict by explaining the case in a nontraditional way.

As you practice the Disciplined Dreaming system, you'll find ways to inject creativity in every setting of your business life, from your Monday morning staff meeting to setting up the trade show booth, from finding a better way to install the tires on a new car to coming up with a new cocktail recipe in the bar of your hotel chain employer. Don't limit the system to product development meetings; think of Disciplined Dreaming as part of your personal and organizational DNA.

Developing Creative Muscle

All humans have muscle mass that can be developed through sustained, structured practice. That's a simple fact: no matter our sex, height, or bone structure, if we hit the gym and start pumping iron, we develop bigger, stronger muscles. Musicians have to develop their muscles, too, to get the sounds they want from their instruments. Fingers, lips, lungs, legs, and arms—you need toned muscular control to master just about any instrument, and that involves practice, practice, and more practice.

Creativity is no different. "Studies have shown that creativity is close to 80 percent learned and acquired," according to Harvard Business School professor Clayton Christensen.[2] I want you to think of your creativity as a muscle and the Disciplined Dreaming system as your ongoing workout system for developing your creative capacity. By making the system a part of your daily routine, you can expect to increase your creative capacity by 20, 30, or even 50 percent. Imagine how much more effective you could be at your job or in your family life with that kind of creative development.

Imagine the edge your company would gain if, together, your team increased its overall creative capacity by even a mere 20 percent.

The Disciplined Dreaming system offers you a variety of exercises to develop your natural characteristics of curiosity, imagination, synthesis, awareness, and memory into strong creative capabilities. Even simple exercises can have powerful results. Inventors leverage their curiosity, for example, by asking questions: Why don't cars have an autopilot feature? What if we lived to be two hundred years old? Why can't every hotel have an automated check-in system?

Aristotle said, "We are what we repeatedly do. Excellence, then, is not an act but a habit." Your creative skills may have grown dormant over the years, and that means you'll need to give them time to develop the habit of creativity. As your skills grow, you'll use the Disciplined Dreaming system to continue to develop and expand your creative capabilities.

Expanding Your Creative Vision

Edward de Bono, sometimes called the father of modern creativity, coined the term *lateral thinking* in the early 1970s. It involves "thinking that seeks new ways of looking at a problem rather than proceeding by logical steps."[3] He used the term to describe a set of approaches and techniques designed to find radically new approaches to problems—to come from the side rather than the front.

Although the Disciplined Dreaming process gives you a step-by-step approach, you will get the most from it if you learn to "look sideways" throughout the process. Here are some tips to consider as you allow your mind to explore in new directions:

- **Tolerate ambiguity.** There will be times when things don't add up or you feel as though you are off track. These are often the situations where you are getting very close to a breakthrough. Keep pushing forward!

- **Avoid "right" and "wrong" answers.** Focus more on the questions—especially open-ended questions—than on the answers.
- **Accept ruts and grooves**. There will be times when you feel as though nothing is clicking, then out of nowhere, the ideas begin to pour out of you. Focus more on the process and on driving curiosity than on trying to force results. The outcomes will happen if you let them.
- **Listen.** Renowned creative director and television producer Lori Weiss believes that listening is the key to creativity. She urges her colleagues to always be open minded and to listen—to what people say, what they don't say, and what the environment is telling them. You will connect to a wellspring of creativity if you clear your mind and listen.[4]
- **Don't be rigid or stubborn.** Your favorite idea may be great, but there may be an even better one if you are willing to accept it. Don't let your experience translate into your being hardwired to the past.
- **Seek input.** The more diverse minds you can deploy against your Creativity Challenge, the more possibilities you will be able to consider. Don't limit your sources to the "experts." Seek input from unrelated fields and different perspectives.

Above all, as you use the Disciplined Dreaming process to expand your creative vision, remember to challenge everything. Challenge assumptions. Challenge the status quo. Challenge the "complacent incumbents." Challenge the rules. Challenge yourself.

Finding a Home in the Messy Process of Creativity

As you work through this book, I hope you will become more comfortable with the sometimes messy process of creativity. Imagine an artist's studio. A painter's loft is rarely the scene of neatly organized rows of paints and tables free of clutter. What might appear at first glance to be a disorganized mess of half-finished projects, time-wasting toys, and scattered tools is, instead, a fertile playground for creativity, improvisation, and the explosive generation of ideas.

The creative process is messy, nonlinear, and abstract. It isn't something that fits neatly in a box or conforms to predictability. Some days are inspired and extremely productive; others seem to achieve few results. Creative bursts may be followed by a lull. As you embark on the Disciplined Dreaming process, you need to give yourself permission to work in the messy, nonlinear environment of creativity.

Remember that you're learning an art, not a manufacturing technique. Jazz artists become better over time not only through the perfection of their craft but also because of increased confidence in their own abilities. As they learn the cycles of their musical creativity, they know that the next creative burst is just around the corner. Over time, these cycles decrease in length, and the low periods become fewer and farther between.

The same thing will happen for you as you nurture and grow your creative capacity. Your experience of overcoming challenges, working through soft spots, and ultimately achieving strong results will not only motivate you to continue but also provide the confidence you'll need to handle the next obstacle. You will end up creating a positive cycle that increases in speed, while your creative work becomes better with each note you play, each melody you compose.

Building Your Creativity Chops: The Self-Assessment

Before you discover your new artistic self, let's get a baseline take on your current creative readiness. The self-assessment you'll complete here goes beyond the activities you'll find in the closing elements of other chapters in the book. This thirty-question test will give you an accurate picture of where you stand today and of what areas you'll need to focus on to grow your creative capacity.

This assessment provides you with your Creativity Baseline Score. It will help you establish where you currently are in your views on creativity, and will also identify specific areas for growth. This isn't the equivalent of a creativity IQ text, and the score doesn't represent the limit of your creative potential. In fact, there is no such thing. Your creativity is virtually limitless, and is something that you can expand and develop throughout your life. Your score in this assessment simply measures where you are right now, not where you can go in the future.

As you go through the following questions, answer on behalf of yourself and your company. Each question offers answers on a 1–5 scale, where 5 represents "strongly agree" and 1 represents "strongly disagree." As you choose your answer to each question, record the number in the scoring chart located at the end of the list of assessment questions.

1. I bring my creativity with me to every meeting and use it in every interaction. It is truly a part of who I am.
   (1) Strongly Disagree (2) Disagree (3) Neutral (4) Agree (5) Strongly Agree

2. Before beginning a project that requires creativity, I always understand clearly what I am trying to accomplish.
   (1) Strongly Disagree (2) Disagree (3) Neutral (4) Agree (5) Strongly Agree

3. I am comfortable sharing my opinion and taking risks at work.
   (1) Strongly Disagree (2) Disagree (3) Neutral (4) Agree (5) Strongly Agree

4. I rarely run out of sources of creativity. I have many sources of inspiration at my disposal.
   (1) Strongly Disagree (2) Disagree (3) Neutral (4) Agree (5) Strongly Agree

5. My colleagues and I feel as though we have too many breakthrough ideas as opposed to not enough.
   (1) Strongly Disagree (2) Disagree (3) Neutral (4) Agree (5) Strongly Agree

6. In my team, the best idea wins, not the person with the fanciest title.
   (1) Strongly Disagree (2) Disagree (3) Neutral (4) Agree (5) Strongly Agree

7. I feel I have a large supply of creativity inside me.
   (1) Strongly Disagree (2) Disagree (3) Neutral (4) Agree (5) Strongly Agree

8. I regularly challenge and question the status quo.
   (1) Strongly Disagree (2) Disagree (3) Neutral (4) Agree (5) Strongly Agree

9. I routinely do warm-up exercises to prepare to unleash my best thinking.
   (1) Strongly Disagree (2) Disagree (3) Neutral (4) Agree (5) Strongly Agree

10. When faced with a creative challenge, I usually can get started quickly and easily.
    (1) Strongly Disagree (2) Disagree (3) Neutral (4) Agree (5) Strongly Agree

11. Brainstorming sessions are frequent, fun, focused, and productive at my company.
    (1) Strongly Disagree (2) Disagree (3) Neutral (4) Agree (5) Strongly Agree

12. We have a system for sorting out the best ideas from the not-as-good ones.
    (1) Strongly Disagree (2) Disagree (3) Neutral (4) Agree (5) Strongly Agree

13. Where I work, creativity is for everyone...not just something those "art" people do.
    (1) Strongly Disagree (2) Disagree (3) Neutral (4) Agree (5) Strongly Agree

14. I often find myself wondering about possibilities and wondering why some things don't currently exist.
    (1) Strongly Disagree (2) Disagree (3) Neutral (4) Agree (5) Strongly Agree

15. When working on new ideas, I leave my normal surroundings and find a physical environment that enables my creativity.
    (1) Strongly Disagree (2) Disagree (3) Neutral (4) Agree (5) Strongly Agree

16. I feel confident enough to tackle any creative challenge, big or small.
    (1) Strongly Disagree (2) Disagree (3) Neutral (4) Agree (5) Strongly Agree

17. When my team and I work to develop new ideas, we use many different and powerful techniques to uncover our best thinking.
    (1) Strongly Disagree (2) Disagree (3) Neutral (4) Agree (5) Strongly Agree

18. I feel that our system for measuring ideas and creativity is sufficient.
    (1) Strongly Disagree (2) Disagree (3) Neutral (4) Agree (5) Strongly Agree

19. Creativity is valued, nurtured, and rewarded in my organization.
    (1) Strongly Disagree (2) Disagree (3) Neutral (4) Agree (5) Strongly Agree

20. I rarely accept things as they are, and often question authority.
    (1) Strongly Disagree (2) Disagree (3) Neutral (4) Agree (5) Strongly Agree

21. As I create new things, I rarely edit as I go.
    (1) Strongly Disagree (2) Disagree (3) Neutral (4) Agree (5) Strongly Agree

22. I have an abundance of techniques for spurring my best thinking.
    (1) Strongly Disagree (2) Disagree (3) Neutral (4) Agree (5) Strongly Agree

23. I have a vivid imagination and often come up with "wacky" ideas.
    (1) Strongly Disagree (2) Disagree (3) Neutral (4) Agree (5) Strongly Agree

24. Once I have a good idea, I usually test it before bringing it to the world.
    (1) Strongly Disagree (2) Disagree (3) Neutral (4) Agree (5) Strongly Agree

25. Creativity, original thought, and imagination are some of my top personal and professional priorities.
    (1) Strongly Disagree (2) Disagree (3) Neutral (4) Agree (5) Strongly Agree

26. I am highly aware of my surroundings and environment.
     (1) Strongly Disagree (2) Disagree (3) Neutral (4) Agree (5) Strongly
     Agree
27. I feel comfortable taking risks and contributing my most innovative
     ideas with no fear of embarrassment or retribution.
     (1) Strongly Disagree (2) Disagree (3) Neutral (4) Agree (5) Strongly
     Agree
28. I regularly use metaphors and analogies.
     (1) Strongly Disagree (2) Disagree (3) Neutral (4) Agree (5) Strongly
     Agree
29. We have a good system in place to generate creative ideas for any type
     of challenge.
     (1) Strongly Disagree (2) Disagree (3) Neutral (4) Agree (5) Strongly
     Agree
30. When we generate good ideas, there is always a clear next step for
     putting them into action.
     (1) Strongly Disagree (2) Disagree (3) Neutral (4) Agree (5) Strongly
     Agree

SCORING

Step 1: List the answer to each question to the right of the corresponding
     number in the chart:

A		B		C		D		E		F	
1		2		3		4		5		6	
7		8		9		10		11		12	
13		14		15		16		17		18	
19		20		21		22		23		24	
25		26		27		28		29		30	
TOTAL:		TOTAL:		TOTAL:		TOTAL:		TOTAL:		TOTAL:	

Your Total Creativity Baseline Score:	

Step 2: Total each of the columns. This will give you a score for columns A,
     B, C, D, E, and F.
Step 3: Add your total scores from each of the five columns to give you
     your total Creativity Baseline Score.

THE RESULTS

Starting with your Creativity Baseline Score, let's take a look at what the results indicate:

130–150: You are in a much better spot than most, as this score puts you in the top 10 percent of creative individuals and companies. You are connected to your creative self and are in an organization that supports it. This score also means that you are well situated to continue to grow your creative capacity and are on your way to reaching your full potential. The techniques and concepts you will learn in this book will be instrumental in helping you further grow your creative capacity and apply your imagination for optimal results.

110–129: Certainly not bad, but you have a lot of room for improvement. This score indicates that you are doing many things right, but also have some significant barriers that are getting in the way of your creativity. You may be in an organization that is inhibiting your creativity and holding you back. This score range should alert you that you have a lot of creative potential but may not be using it effectively. You will grow tremendously by putting the Disciplined Dreaming process to work for the benefit of your company and yourself.

85–109: Unfortunately, you are in the same situation as nearly 60 percent of the business population. You probably have great creative abilities, but they are being significantly restricted most of the time. You are probably frustrated with the bureaucracy of your organization or have a number of limiting beliefs that are holding you back from expressing your true creative abilities. You may tell yourself such stories as "I'm not creative" or "I can't share by ideas because people will laugh at me." Your creativity muscles need to be dusted off and given a rigorous workout. The good news is that you will see immediate and tremendous growth by using the Disciplined Dreaming system. You are about to unlock creativity you didn't even know you had, and will enjoy an exciting new way of approaching the world.

84 or less: You are in the creativity danger zone. This score should serve as a loud wake-up call to you and your organization; it should signal that something must be changed or you will run into significant problems moving forward. You are a lost creative soul and need to immediately reconnect with your imagination. Your organization is holding you back, and you need to become a change agent to reshape your company or find a new one. Although this information may be alarming, don't get too discouraged. You are about to go through a transformational change by putting the Disciplined Dreaming process to work. You will immediately enjoy a boost in your creativity and have a lot of fun in the process. It will push you outside your comfort zone, so please remember that that's the only place where real growth happens.

Keep in mind that your score is an indication of where you currently are situated compared to your creative potential, but it is not in any way a reflection of that potential. The score simply tells you where you and your organization currently sit and serves as a starting point on your creative journey.

Now let's take a look at your subscores. The scores for each column, lettered A through F, indicate some specific areas where you currently show strengths or weaknesses. Each of these subscores has a maximum point value of 25. Here's how the point values break down:

22–25	Excellent
19–21	Above average
17–18	Average
16 or less	Below average

The score for each column represents a different element of your creative capacity:

Column A: The questions in this column correspond to general characteristics about the creative readiness of you and your company.

Column B: This score indicates how you are doing in terms of vision, curiosity, and awareness—issues you will address in step 1 of the Disciplined Dreaming process, Ask.

Column C: The questions in this column correspond to issues you will address in step 2 of the Disciplined Dreaming process, Prepare. This score shows how well you prepare your environment and mind-set to unleash your best ideas.

Column D: The questions in this column correspond to step 3 of the Disciplined Dreaming process, Discover. Your score here indicates your ability to find creative ideas and inspiration in many different areas of life.

Column E: The questions in this column correspond to step 4 of the Disciplined Dreaming process, Ignite. This score indicates how adept you are at generating ample high-quality ideas when needed.

Column F: The questions in this column correspond to step 5 of the Disciplined Dreaming process, Launch. Your score shows how well you are able to sort out the best ideas and then put that creativity into action.

Remember, these scores give you a peek in the mirror and offer some perspective of where you are today and which areas need the most focus for growth. Keep that information in mind as you take your first steps into the Disciplined Dreaming process.

STEP ONE

———●———

ASK

3

•

Defining the Creativity Challenge

In the long run, men hit only what they aim at.
—HENRY DAVID THOREAU

The first step of the Disciplined Dreaming process is to define your Creativity Challenge—the specific problem you want to solve. As the old saying goes, "You'll never hit a target you cannot see." The more clearly and thoroughly you detail your Creativity Challenge, the more effective you'll be at resolving it. Think of your Creativity Challenge as the image on the box cover of a jigsaw puzzle. Without that image, you would have an extremely difficult time solving the puzzle. By studying it, you know exactly what the solution will look like, and you can determine specifically how to connect the pieces before you to achieve the solution. Your Creativity Challenge will offer you that same type of guidance in achieving your objectives.

Throughout the Disciplined Dreaming process, you will direct your creativity toward this clearly defined objective, so it's important that you thoroughly detail your Creativity Challenge in this first step. To reveal those details, you'll complete a Creativity Brief—a series of questions that will help you "fill in the blanks" as you define your Creativity Challenge. Asking yourself and your team these critical questions up front brings the Disciplined Dreaming process to life and enables you to direct your creativity with purpose.

Building the Creativity Brief

David Sable is a prolific marketer. As the vice chairman and chief operating officer of Wunderman, the largest direct marketing agency in the world, he has been the creative genius behind dozens of the most successful campaigns for Ford, Microsoft, Citibank, and Hewlett-Packard. Among advertising professionals, he is known worldwide for his creativity and vision and is an inspiration to up-and-coming execs.

David and his team start every campaign with a Creative Brief. This document, an established protocol in advertising, helps direct the team's creativity toward a specific objective. The Creative Brief specifies important aspects of the project objectives, the brand, and the client, while serving as a guidepost to help the team members coordinate their efforts. Common elements include the following:

- *Overview:* a description of the project and what problem the client is trying to solve.
- *History:* What has led up to this point? What has been tried before, and what were the results? What impact will this background have on the project?
- *Objective:* What specific outcome is the client trying to accomplish? How will success be measured?
- *Deliverables:* What is the physical output that is due at the end of the project (a TV commercial, a new positioning statement, a new logo)?
- *Target audience:* Whom will this message reach? What do we know about this audience, and how can we tailor the messages appropriately?
- *Timeline:* specific due dates for milestones throughout the project as well as a final completion date.

- *Client:* Who are the key decision makers, and specifically which people must provide approval at each stage of the project?
- *Budget:* What financial constraints must be adhered to?

For David's team and others in advertising, these briefs make projects go much more smoothly and their results much more effective. A brief allows all vested parties to be on the same page in terms of vision, plan, execution, and expectations. Without it, people's work would probably be disjointed and miss the mark. The brief enables creativity while keeping things running efficiently.

In Disciplined Dreaming, the *Creativity Brief* is a similar tool you can apply to make any creative pursuit more successful. By providing a system for organizing your thoughts up front, the Creativity Brief will serve as your North Star and guide you toward the best possible creative outcome.

Warning: the Creativity Brief is intense and will take real work to complete. But that work is a good investment. By taking the time up front to get it right, you will yield an exponentially better end result. This document will also be an important "sales" tool for getting buy-in for your creative ideas from bosses, CFOs, team leaders, and others who may need to authorize the project or approve steps along the way.

Remember, the structure of this system is there to support— not limit—your creativity. Like most elements of the Disciplined Dreaming process, the Creativity Brief is flexible. Depending on the size of your Creativity Challenge, you may not need to answer every single question. Use your judgment to complete as much as you will need before embarking on your creative project. At the end of this chapter, you'll find a "reduced calorie," simpler version of the Creativity Brief to use for smaller Creativity Challenges. Now let's review each of the sections included in the full Creativity Brief, as shown here.

The Creativity Brief

Project Name:
Date Started:
Date Due:
Team Members:

I.   Describing the Desired Outcome (in One Sentence)
II.   Defining the Creativity Challenge
    a. What is the problem you are solving for?
    b. Can you restate it in a few different ways? What about reversing it?
    c. Write twenty questions about your challenge.
    d. What is the need for change?
    e. What value is created by doing something new?
    f.   What is a simile for the challenge?
    g. Can you establish a "spine"? If so, what is it?
    h. List key observations and assumptions about the challenge.
    i.   Could you paint a picture or make a model of the challenge?
III. Situation Analysis
    a. Past:
        What worked and didn't work, and why?
        What consequences have occurred?
        What baggage exists?
    b. Present:
        What are you currently doing?
        What is conventional wisdom?
        What is the status quo, and who is trying to protect it?
    c. Future:
        What does the ideal solution look like for this challenge?
        How will the world be better if you get this right?
        What difference will a great outcome have on your company, your career, or both?
IV.   The Resistance
    a. People: Who would lose if this problem were solved?

Section I: Describing the Desired Outcome

Your first task is to write a *one-sentence* description of the desired outcome of your Creativity Challenge. Brevity is the tricky part: it will force you to refine your thinking and be concise. You need to ask

      b. Obstacles: list the roadblocks that may get in your way.

      c. Costs: What are the financial considerations that could limit your creativity?

      d. What do you and your team fear?

      e. Complete this sentence: We would be completely successful in this effort if only . . .

V.   Target Audience(s)

      a. Whom is the idea for?

      b. Whom do you need to convince?

      c. Once implemented, whom will this idea impact?

VI. Communication Strategy

      a. How will you communicate to others about the idea?

      b. Will you seek feedback along the way or keep it quiet until launch?

      c. What is your plan to roll out the idea once complete?

VII. Competition

      a. Who else is trying to solve this same challenge right now?

      b. Are there competitive ideas?

      c. Is your idea competing with other Creativity Challenges for resources?

VIII. Project Plan

      a. Break the Creativity Challenge into smaller mini-challenges to make it easier to manage.

      b. Establish the tone and style of the project.

      c. List the rules of the road—the dos and don'ts.

      d. Set specific deliverables or outputs you expect from taking this Creativity Challenge.

      e. Establish the budget.

      f. Create a timeline including key milestone dates and the people responsible for various tasks along the way.

IX. Key Metrics

      a. How will you define success?

      b. List three to five key performance indicators (KPIs) for measuring the success of your Creativity Challenge.

      c. If everything goes well, what level of return on investment could you realize?

yourself, "In a perfect world, what am I trying to accomplish?" Make sure not to limit yourself with how you will achieve this outcome, what it will cost, who needs to approve it, and so on. Right now it is all about defining what an ideal victory would look like. For example: "Invent a product enhancement that increases our market share from 31 percent to 38 percent" or "Decrease production time by eleven hours."

Section II: Defining the Creativity Challenge

a.   **What is the problem you are solving for?** In math, you are often asked to "solve for x." The same concept applies here. What is the key issue that needs changing or improvement? It could be a large problem, such as curing a disease, or a much smaller problem, such as how to clean the lobby with fewer supplies. The most important aspect is to clearly articulate the problem you are working to solve.

b.   **Can you restate it in a few different ways? What about reversing it?** By looking at the problem from different vantage points, you will build a deeper understanding of the problem and uncover more opportunities for solving it. You may find it very helpful to refer back to this section periodically as you continue through the creative process.

c.   **Write twenty questions about your challenge.** Nothing spurs the imagination like asking questions. Play this version of Twenty Questions to really connect with the details of the problem. You may ask, for example, Where did this problem come from? Who created it, and who tried to solve it before? How much is this problem costing us on an annual basis? What will happen if we do nothing about this problem? How is this problem impacting the culture and morale of our team? How is our competition thinking about this problem?

d.   **What is the need for change?** Creating the case for change is critical to securing buy-in, funding, and acceptance for your new solution. You need to think through why this is the right problem to be solving in the first place, and why it must be addressed now. Ideally, you will create urgency around the problem and clearly articulate the need for change.

e.   **What value is created by doing something new?** Is it worth it? That's the underlying question here. How will a change add new value in any form (financial, health, social impact, helping people, and so on)?

f.   **What is a simile for the challenge?** Have some fun with this one. Complete the sentence, "My challenge is like a . . . " A good simile can be a very helpful tool, not only in coming up with new ideas but also in explaining them. Is your challenge like trying to become the "Microsoft of plumbing supplies"? Are you in the same crunch as a football team that is down by ten points in the final minutes of the fourth quarter? Is there a famous quote that describes your problem, such as "Chase two rabbits and both will escape," that might be a simile for the missed opportunities of an unfocused team? One note of caution: similes can be very helpful, but only use them in broad strokes, to convey tone or scope. Don't get locked into them: you'll end up following the existing story instead of creating your own.

g.   **Can you establish a "spine" for your Creativity Challenge? If so, what is it?** In *The Creative Habit,* choreographer Twyla Tharp shares the concept of a *spine* as the central analogy or backbone of a piece of work. For example, one of her works of dance and music could have the underlying story of Romeo and Juliet as its spine. The spine may be apparent to the audience (as with Vivaldi's masterpiece *The Four Seasons*), or it may be hidden from obvious view. The key point here is that identifying a spine—a central element or theme—for your Creativity Challenge can help your creative process take shape and form as you explore new ideas. For example, "All product names for our new line of laptop computers will be those of predatory animals."

h.   **List key observations and assumptions about the challenge.** We all enter new territory with preconceptions. In this section of the Creativity Brief, brainstorm a list of your observations and assumptions about the challenge. The more you list, the better. This will help raise your awareness of both the problem and how you already view it. It will help you break through prejudices and find new, compelling solutions.

i.   **Could we paint a picture or make a model of the challenge?** Different people process information in different ways. The more you and your team immerse all of your senses in the problem, the better your ultimate results will be. By describing your challenge through another medium (besides words on the page)—whether expressing it visually through color and paints, tactilely with a three-dimensional model, or even orally by writing a rap song—approaching it through different senses can help you connect more strongly to the essence of the problem and lead to fresh creativity as you embark on the rest of the Disciplined Dreaming process.

Section III: Situation Analysis

a.   **The past.** To get a good grip on the situation, it is helpful to first look to the past. Examine the approaches that have been tried in the past. What was successful? What failed, and why? This clarity will help you avoid previous mistakes and break free from preconceived notions.

b.   **The present.** How are you currently dealing with the situation or problem? It is important to examine conventional wisdom and the status quo so that you know how to differentiate new approaches. It is also good to understand whom the status quo benefits, and who is likely to try to protect it. You should also take a look at how your competitors are dealing with this problem, and how other people in other industries may be proceeding. Is there a comparative issue in the nonprofit world that you could learn from? What about the entertainment industry or government or marine biology? Framing the current situation from a number of perspectives will be helpful.

c.   **The future.** If you had unlimited time, money, and resources, what would the ideal solution to the challenge look like? By solving this challenge, what would the tangible benefits be, and how will you make the world a better place? Also explore the impact this solution would have on your company and your career. Is it a game-changer or an incremental improvement? Not to say that one is better than the other, but it is helpful to know if you are trying to knock a grand-slam home run out of the park or if you are just trying to get on base.

Section IV: The Resistance

Resistance will come in many forms. In this section, you'll identify the people, costs, fears, and other obstacles you and your team must face in order to resolve your Creativity Challenge. There are likely to be people who are deeply invested in the status quo and will fight you aggressively against change. There may be internal obstacles, customer issues, regulatory challenges, or even social norms in your organization that may seem hard to break. You'll also look at the economics at hand, to uncover any cost issues that could throw you off track.

Fear is the biggest inhibitor of creativity, and in Chapter Eight, you'll learn several techniques for conquering it. As you work through this section of the Creativity Brief, remember that change is scary for us all, but often our best life sits on the other side of our fears. Although it may feel awkward, hold a quick brainstorming session with your team to list all your collective fears about the project. By identifying them up front in one "fear list" and agreeing not to allow them to hold you back, you are giving yourself and your team permission to push the boundaries and let your creativity soar.

Finally, you will identify the "if onlys"—the greatest issues that stand between you and achieving your creative solution. Identifying these if-onlys is another powerful technique to help guide your creative process. It's easy to get bogged down in the excuses and reasons for why we can't do something remarkable and, as a result, to end up settling for a third-rate idea. By listing and then removing the if-onlys, you will free yourself up for full creative expression.

Section V: Target Audience(s)

Successfully launching a new idea is likely to require an act of persuasion. You may need to seek budgetary approval from your boss to further explore your idea. You may need to convince a vendor to send your supplies. You may need to sell that ornery line manager to implement your new time-saving idea. If your Creativity Challenge is related to a product, you will certainly need to persuade your customers to buy. Even if you are a solo act, you'll still need to convince yourself to move forward with purpose.

Because all new ideas require some selling, getting in touch with your audience is critical. Identifying the key players up front will help direct your creativity to the most effective results. You will want to examine who needs to approve your idea, whom it will impact if implemented, who will possibly object to it, and whose buy-in you need to execute it.

Section VI: Communication Strategy

a. **How will you communicate to others about the idea?** You should think in advance about the way you will be communicating. Will it be weekly e-mail updates? Storyboards? Review meetings? Remember that too many people weighing in early can water down your ideas, so you may want to develop your concepts into something tangible before sharing them.

b. **Will you seek feedback along the way or keep it quiet until launch?** This can be a tough question to answer. On the one hand, you may want buy-in, input, and perhaps approval to move forward.

On the other hand, fully developing an idea and doing a big rollout can be advantageous in the right circumstances. There's no right or wrong answer here, so it really depends on the specific situation surrounding your Creativity Challenge.

c.   **What is your plan to roll out the idea once complete?** Keeping your target audiences in mind, what will be the most effective way to unleash the idea? The answer could range from conducting a full-scale, worldwide consumer media blitz to posting your new concept on the tack board in the coffee room. Considering your rollout options in advance can help guide your thinking through the creative process.

Section VII: Competition

a.   **Who else is trying to solve this same challenge right now?** Are there other teams at your own company addressing the same issue? Perhaps there are competitors in the marketplace working on the same problem. Competitors could be corporations, universities, government agencies, nonprofits, or even individual citizens. Pull together a list of others who are working on the same project so that you can explore potential opportunities for collaborating—rather than competing—with them. For example, maybe you could team up with a nonprofit organization trying to solve the same problem; together you would be devoting more resources to solving it.

b.   **Are there competitive ideas?** You may want to pursue a particular way to solve a certain challenge and find that there are other, competitive approaches already being considered to solve the same problem. Another option is to see if combining your idea with an existing proposed idea generates a third, better idea. Even if your fiercest competitors are working on a similar issue, it is better to learn everything you can about how they are approaching the challenge. As the old saying goes, "Keep your friends close and your enemies closer."

c. **Is your idea competing with other Creativity Challenges for resources?** You may have no direct competition for your specific Creativity Challenge, but you could be competing with other challenges for the same support, money, time, facility space, raw materials, research grants, or people. Consider what you will need to launch your idea and then think through what other ideas are fighting for those same resources.

Section VIII: Project Plan

a. **Break the Creativity Challenge into smaller mini-challenges to make it easier to manage.** How do you eat an elephant? One bite at a time, as the saying goes. Depending on the size of your project, you may be able to break your Creativity Challenge into smaller, "bite-sized" challenges that are easier to develop and manage. You'll need to use your judgment here, but my suggestion is that if you can break it down into smaller chunks, do it. Think of it as composing your jazz masterpiece one note at a time.

b. **Establish the tone and style of the project.** Discuss with your team what the style of the project is. Are you trying to come up with an irreverent, racy solution or something that must fit into a stodgy bureaucracy? The more you can develop the feel of the project, the better able you will be to direct your thinking.

c. **List the rules of the road—the dos and don'ts.** When you are driving, you can choose your lane and your route, but you are not allowed to blow through red lights, drive beyond the speed limit, or go the wrong direction down a one-way street. What are the rules of engagement in your situation? Are there specific rules that must be followed, such as regulatory mandates, laws, safety constraints, policies, or charters? Even if your idea ultimately will break some rules, it's good to know what lines you'll cross in the process.

d.   **Set specific deliverables or outputs you expect from taking this Creativity Challenge**. You need to define what you actually plan to deliver as part of your creative process. How will your idea be represented? Will it be a business case? A diagram? A working model? A video, Web site, song, poem, blog, dance, or rap? A PowerPoint sales tool for use with investors? A memo to the board of directors? Even though the main objective is to generate the best idea, you will want to think about the possible ways that the idea will ultimately take shape and be delivered.

e.   **Establish the budget.** You may be working inside an existing constraint or have access to tremendous resources. Whatever the case, just be sure to set the budget up front and stick to it. Your brilliant ideas will be overshadowed if you blow through your resources and ignore the financial implications of your creativity.

f.   **Create a timeline including key milestone dates and the people responsible for various tasks along the way.** Here you'll develop a detailed timeline that includes specific milestones and the names of people responsible for delivering them, to make sure everyone's expectations are in sync. By clearly defining roles, you will earn the support of your organization and secure the resources you need to unleash your best ideas.

Section IX: Key Metrics

a.   **How will you define success?** Success for a Creativity Challenge can come in many forms. There are tangible examples, such as monetary (earn $5 million of incremental profit per quarter), environmental (improve air quality by 11 percent), efficiency (reduce processing costs by 5.6 percent), quality (decrease defect rate to 1:10,000), or time (cut production cycles by three days). There are also intangible goals you may be striving for, such as improving the aesthetics of your work environment, creating joy and camaraderie, or helping people become more supportive corporate citizens. You need to assign some form of measurement to your goals, no matter how intangible they might seem. For example, you could measure "joy and camaraderie" by conducting a survey before your idea launches and then doing the same survey afterwards. The more closely you can define the specific results you are trying to achieve, the better directed your creative thinking will be.

b.   **List three to five key performance indicators (KPIs) for measuring the success of your Creativity Challenge**. Your friends in the finance or strategic planning departments will love this. KPI is a business buzzword that basically refers to numbers on a dashboard. Your car's KPIs, for example, include fuel consumption, average speed, and RPMs. The KPIs for your Creativity Challenge will represent the most important measures related to your goal. If you are trying to launch a new flavor of cereal, KPIs may include customer satisfaction rating, take-rate (percentage of consumer selection of this product versus competing products), cost per ounce, and shipping time.

c.   **If everything goes well, what level of return on investment could you realize?** A pretty straightforward question, but one of the most important ones you need to ask in order to receive funding and support for the project. If you believe that the fully loaded cost (including all actual costs, people costs, time costs, facility and overhead costs, research costs, and opportunity costs) to develop your idea is $10,000, for example, how much profit do you think the idea could generate? Obviously this is a tough question to answer because you don't even have the idea yet, but thinking through a range could be very helpful. If you get the idea right and your $10,000 investment could be worth $5 million, this is a pretty good indication that your idea is worth pursuing and investing in. In contrast, if a total success would generate only $13,000 of profit, you may want to spend your time on a different Creativity Challenge.

FERRER-ORTIZ
JULIO C

Wed May 29 2013

Disciplined dreaming : a proven

33029090300559

Hold note:

*
*
*
*
*
*
*
*
*
*
*
*
*
*

Hold note

33005808030002280

Please return to ... a proven

Wed May 29 2013

JULIO C
FERRER-ORTIZ

Bringing Discipline to Your Dreams Through Vision, Clarity, and Action

With your Creativity Brief complete, you have covered a lot of the disciplined work that makes creativity possible. As labor-intensive as some of this groundwork can be, it is essential to unleashing your highest creative potential. Just as a key signature or tempo provides structure for a jazz band, your Creativity Brief will be your guide to vision, clarity, and action as you resolve your Creativity Challenge.

In 1976, Ed Catmull and John Lasseter launched Pixar with a clear vision. They wanted to reinvent the animated motion picture industry by introducing lifelike computer-generated images. This was a clear, unambiguous goal in their minds, and it helped them stay focused. This vision was realized with such blockbuster successes as *Toy Story* (1994), *Monsters, Inc.* (2001), *Finding Nemo* (2003), and *Cars* (2006). As a result of their relentless pursuit of their vision over a twenty-five-year period, the studio earned twenty-two Academy Awards, six Golden Globes, and three Grammys. In 2006, Pixar was sold to Disney, the previous king of animation, for $7.4 billion, and Pixar's owners became the largest shareholder of the Walt Disney Company.[1]

Having a clear sense of the ultimate outcome you desire and a clear definition of your ultimate destination point will help you chart the best course, but, as Rabindranath Tagore, the nineteenth-century Indian poet, novelist, and playwright said, "You can't cross the sea merely by standing and staring at the water."[2] Now you are ready to take action. In the next chapter, you'll find some specific ideas and activities for driving curiosity, to help you and your team as you work to define your Creativity Challenge and complete the Creativity Brief. As you move to later steps in the Disciplined Dreaming process, you may encounter unforeseen twists and turns—you may even end up reshaping your Creativity Challenge along the way. The important thing is to lay the groundwork with as much vision and clarity as you can and then begin the creative journey.

Building Your Creativity Chops

The Disciplined Dreaming process is designed to ignite both your left brain (logical, analytical) and your right brain (creative, abstract). The accountant meets the artist. The engineer meets the poet. We've covered a detailed, analytical approach to clearly articulate the Creativity Challenge. Here are some ideas, activities, and tools you and your team can use to connect with a Creativity Challenge in a nontraditional way.

1. **Name that ship.** Sitting with your team, go around the room and have people take turns naming a type of ship, to see how long it takes for people to make creative leaps. Here's how it is likely to go: "cruise ship," "battleship," "tugboat," "freight ship," "speedboat." Then someone will cross into new territory: "spaceship," "rocket ship." This realization will spark yet another creative leap: "relationship," "friendship," "courtship." Continue for a few more rounds to see how abstract the group can get. This is a great warm-up for any creativity session.

2. **Creative visualization**. There is great power in deeply tuning in to what you are trying to create. Engage each of your five senses to fully visualize the ultimate solution to your Creativity Challenge. What would it look like? Feel like? Sound like? Smell like? Taste like? The more emotionally connected and

viscerally you feel the desired outcome, the closer you are to achieving it.

3. **Zooming out**. Zoom out to take a "satellite view" of your challenge. To do that, you'll need to get rid of assumptions, which is easier said than done. For example, if your challenge were to find a new way to clean teeth, you would most likely begin working on an innovative new type of toothbrush. But what about a liquid cleaning solution? Or self-cleaning gum? Or a professional teeth-cleaning service sold by membership in a club? By really examining the problem you are trying to solve from a big-picture perspective, you'll end up keeping your options open for more creativity throughout the process.

4. **Death by questions**. Dr. Hal Gregersen, professor of leadership at INSEAD, a leading international graduate school of business, recommends identifying a problem and writing nothing but questions about it for ten minutes a day for thirty days. He says that over that period the questions will change, and so will your understanding and approach to the problem.[3] You can use Gregersen's process to help fully explore the ideas and issues surrounding your Creativity Challenge.

5. **Go light**. As you define your Creativity Challenge, think about which type of creativity you are invoking. As I mentioned earlier, if you're shooting for a small act of Everyday Creativity rather than a High-Value Change or Breakthrough Innovation, you may not need to complete all of the steps outlined in the full Creativity Brief. For those types of smaller projects, consider using the Creativity Brief Lite I've included here. You can complete this version in about an hour and still produce a great framework from which to build creative solutions.

Creativity Brief Lite

Project Name:
Date Started:
Date Due:

I.   Describing the Desired Outcome (in One Sentence)
II.   Defining the Creativity Challenge
      a. What is the problem you are solving for?
      b. What is the need for change at all?
      c. What is a simile for the challenge?
      d. List key observations and assumptions about the challenge.
III. Situation Analysis
      a. Past: What worked and didn't work, and why?
      b. Present: What are you currently doing?
      c. Future: What does the ideal solution look like for this challenge?
IV.   The Resistance
      a. People: Who would lose if this problem were solved?
      b. Obstacles: list the roadblocks that may get in your way.
      c. Costs: What are the financial considerations that could limit your
         creativity?
V.   Target Audience(s)
      a. Whom is the idea for?
      b. Whom do you need to convince?
VI.   Communication Strategy
      a. How will you communicate to others about the idea?
VII. Competition
      a. Who else is trying to solve this same challenge right now?
VIII. Project Plan
      a. Set specific deliverables and outputs you expect from taking this Creativity
         Challenge.
      b. Establish the budget.
      c. Create a timeline including key milestone dates and the people respon-
         sible for various tasks along the way.
IX.   Key Metrics
      a. How will you define success?
      b. If everything goes well, what level of return on investment could you
         realize?

4

---•---

Driving Curiosity and Awareness

Curiosity is the most powerful thing you own.

—JAMES CAMERON

"Why do socks always come in pairs of two?" asked Arielle Eckstut. "And why do they have to match? And be boring and plain? What if we did something completely different?"

This curious entrepreneur from New York launched and built Little MissMatched, an incredibly successful business that she originally conceived to sell socks to preteen girls. Most people crazy enough to enter this market would first think about sourcing socks from the lowest-cost factory in China and then figure out how to sell them to Walmart, twelve pair for a dollar. Arielle took a very different approach.

She began by thinking about socks from a user's perspective. If a customer loses one sock, the pair is rendered useless, she realized. That's why you can't buy a "pair" of socks from Little MissMatched; instead, you are welcome to buy a set of three, five, or seven. The socks within these sets are coordinated in color and style, but none of them are exact matches. That's the fun of Little MissMatched. The socks are whimsical, cool, and different, providing customers an element of creative expression in addition to fulfilling a utilitarian function.

Arielle's curiosity led to a creative breakthrough that translated into business success. Within four years of operation, sales leaped to $25 million (that's a lot of socks!), and were projected to continue to grow at 100 percent per year. The company raised $17 million for growth, landed a deal with Macy's to have eighty-five Little Miss-Matched boutiques inside retail stores, and has expanded its products to include adult socks, mittens, and even bedding and furniture.

Little MissMatched questioned the established rules of engagement and challenged existing assumptions about how socks should look, be packaged, and sold. During step 1 of the Disciplined Dreaming process, you use the same sense of curiosity and awareness to drive your own creativity. In this chapter, I've compiled some of my favorite activities, ideas, and techniques for fueling imagination, curiosity, and creative energy.

Asking the Three Magic Questions

Three simple questions can lead you to more (and more astounding) breakthroughs. Tape these to the walls, make them into a screen saver, and tattoo them on your teammates:

1. Why?
2. What if?
3. Why not?

Most of us have become trained to avoid challenging authority, especially at work, so we fail to ask these basic yet powerful questions. To encourage fresh thinking, you need to ask them constantly and make them part of your daily routine. In the same way that you bring a pen and paper to every meeting, make sure to bring these questions to drive curiosity and awareness, which are the building blocks of creativity.

These questions can help you address issues of any size, and you can certainly use them when tackling your Creativity Challenge. Asking "Why?" helps you understand the current state of affairs and challenge the status quo and conventional wisdom. When you ask "What if?" you are exploring fresh possibilities and imagining how the world would look if you made a change or if a new idea came to life. Asking "Why not?" helps you understand constraints. It allows you to connect with the limiting factors that are currently blocking positive change. Here are a few examples of all three types of questions:

Why?

Why are rental car lines so long?

Why do people wait until it rains to buy an umbrella?

Why is the normal workweek forty hours?

Why do some brands command a price premium while others do not?

Why did my favorite TV show get cancelled?

Why do people overeat even when they know the dangers of obesity?

Why is classical music less popular than rap?

Why do we always start and end our meetings five minutes late?

Why did our competitor beat us to market with that great new product feature?

Why do traffic patterns change from city to city?

What If?

What if we charged for our product as a subscription instead of charging a per-unit fee?

What if the stock market increases by 15 percent this year?

What if we could create a candy that actually had "negative" calories that helped people lose weight?

What if the police presence doubled in our city?

What if we eliminated all meetings at our company?
What if the legal drinking age was reduced to eighteen?
What if a retail store had special checkout lanes for premium customers only?

What's Your Color?

In 1981, if you wanted to start a groundbreaking business, one where you could express your creativity and beat your competitors, I bet you wouldn't have chosen the nail polish industry. Going head-to-head with such established giants as Maybelline and Max Factor, who ruled the industry at that time, would have been considered crazy. But George Schaeffer believed that creativity could differentiate his new company even in the highly competitive world of cosmetics. He launched his new company, OPI, and he's been beating the odds ever since.[1]

George questioned the status quo. While other nail products were sold at drug stores and department chains, he sold his products only through salons. He also asked the Three Magic Questions to create new and more exciting names for his nail polish colors. *Why* do the names of colors have to be boring? *What if* we developed names that were fun, romantic, and mysterious instead of boring? None of the competitors sell adventure and intrigue; *why not*?

By 2004, OPI had become the world's largest professional nail-care outfit, boasting $105 million in revenue. Its various collections represent exotic and romantic places around the world, such as the Mexico Collection or the South Beach Collection. Instead of the boring names competitors used, such as "bright pink" or "dark red," OPI's names are a riot. Some favorites include

- I'm Not Really a Waitress
- We'll Always Have Paris
- Lincoln Park After Dark
- Your Cabana or Mine?
- Yes, I Can-Can
- Keys to My Karma
- Text Me? Text You!

By questioning conventional wisdom and challenging the status quo, OPI went on to become a tremendous success. Its original sparks of curiosity led to a new approach to distribution and product names that broke through a mature, commoditized business and led to great results. If upending the status quo and asking the Three Magic Questions can create groundbreaking change in the nail polish industry, just think what they can do for yours.

What if there were no trees?

What if all tax deductions were eliminated?

What if gasoline was $11 per gallon?

Why Not?

Very few men become nurses. Why not?

The number of books read each year by the average American is declining. Why isn't it increasing?

Why not offer our customers free car washes when they buy a new car from our dealership?

People in my company don't often share controversial ideas. Why not?

Questioning existing norms and challenging yourself and your team to explore the possibilities will help you uncover your creative potential. Apply these questions—Why? What if? and Why not?—liberally and with great frequency in as many settings as possible. You might annoy a few bureaucrats, but you'll also tap into an endless supply of imagination.

Making Meatloaf

At ePrize, we often tell the Meatloaf Story. A mother is making meatloaf with her teenage daughter, a ritual they've been doing together for years. As part of the tradition, the two chefs cut the end off one side of the meatloaf before putting it in the oven. One day, the teen asks, "Mom, why do we cut the end off the meatloaf before we put it in the oven?"

Taken by surprise, the mom began to think. She had no good reason, other than that's how her own mother made meatloaf. Together, the two called up Grandma to find the answer. After a brief laugh, the grandmother admitted that she didn't know the answer, either; she'd learned the technique from her mother. Their curiosity sparked, the three went to visit Great-Grandma in the nursing home where she lived. Upon hearing the question, the ninety-eight-year-old great grandmother roared with laughter. "I have no idea why *you* are cutting the end off the meatloaf! I used to do it because I didn't have a big enough pan!"

We use the meatloaf metaphor to define an out-of-date tradition—a system, process, or belief that may have made sense in the past but is no longer relevant. Unfortunately, most companies are filled with meatloaves. Use this story to help remind you to question the status quo and to shed light on long-standing traditions that have no real function or benefit. By awakening your curiosity, you will be amazed at how many you discover.

Opening Your Beginner's Mind

An exceptionally bright student was training to become a monk with a master at a Zen monastery in Japan. The student was a bit arrogant and liked to show off his knowledge to other students. One day, the master sat down with the student for tea. The master poured tea into the student's cup until it ran over, and the tea spilled over the table.

"Master!" cried the student. "Can't you see the cup is already full and cannot accept any more tea?"

"Exactly," said the master. "Just like you, so full of ideas that you cannot accept any new ones. You must approach your study with an 'empty cup' so you leave room to accept new ideas. How can you accept anything new if your cup is already full?"

This story illustrates a concept known in Eastern philosophy as having a *beginner's mind*—a mind that remains completely open to new concepts. As people progress in life (and their careers), they

Scheduling "Heads-Up" Time

We've all heard people in the business world proclaim that they are "heads-down" on a project—so deeply focused that they must tune out the entire world. Step 1 of the Disciplined Dreaming process, Ask, is all about being heads-*up*. Compare the two states of being:

Heads-Down	Heads-Up
Focused on delivery	Focused on possibilities
Tuning out distractions	Embracing new things
Avoiding influence from your surroundings	Welcoming outside influence
Execution	Curiosity and awareness
Getting things done	Questioning everything
Focused on right now	Focused on the future
Asking "What is?"	Asking "What could be?"
Meeting deadlines	Building imagination

There is a time and place for both approaches. When you are working to ship a new product out the door, you'd better hope your team is in full heads-down mode. The problem is that when we spend so much of our time in the heads-down state of mind, it becomes difficult for us to shift into a heads-up position. It is even more difficult trying to bounce back and forth between the two.

The urgency of heads-down demands usually trumps the longer-term importance of being heads-up, so people rarely visit this critical vantage point. As you embark on your Creativity Challenge, make sure to proactively schedule some heads-up time for your team, and hold each other accountable not only for grammatical errors on a memo but, more important, for being curious, aware, and open to new possibilities that can unleash imagination and creativity.

become filled with preconceived notions, assumptions, and history that can cloud their thinking.

To spur curiosity, you want to develop your beginner's mind. As you embark on the creative process, for example, shake things up. Change reading habits, patterns, food, music, the route you take to the office, sleeping habits, and anything else you can think of. These changes will raise your awareness and help you connect with the world in fresh ways. Now let's take a look at six other tools—ideas and actions you can use to nurture your beginner's mind by kicking your curiosity (and your team's) into high gear.

The Big Box

Acclaimed choreographer Twyla Tharp starts every new project with a cardboard box.[2] While she is developing her ideas, she fills the box with anything and everything that could lead to inspiration. The contents can include magazine articles, photos, matchbook covers, songs, toys, fabric, and even food. Tharp views the box as her creative garden, and she plants many seeds in it so that she will be able to enjoy a great harvest. Putting together a Big Box is a wonderful technique for gathering ideas to address your Creativity Challenge. Not only will the contents spark individual curiosity, but you may find interesting links between the items that help you generate fresh ideas.

The Five Whys

This is one of my favorite techniques for getting right to the heart of an issue. As the name suggests, you ask five "why" questions in a row. In other words, when you have an answer to your first "why" question, ask a "why" question about that answer, and then repeat (at least) four times. Here's an example:

1. Q: "Why do our customers prefer our competitor's potato chips instead of ours?" A: "Because they taste better."
2. Q: "Why?" A: "Because they use better seasonings"
3. Q: "Why?" A: "Because they have a better head chef than we do."

4. Q: "Why?" A: "Because we didn't put as much effort into recruiting a new one, and still have the same mediocre head chef from twenty-five years ago."

5. Q: "Why?" A: "Because no one was willing to take a stand and make a case for change to our CEO, and now we are losing market share."

It might make you feel like a four-year-old, but this is one of the most powerful exercises you can use to uncover new ideas and drive curiosity.

Zoom!

Most cameras these days have a zoom capability. The best ones allow you to zoom way in and get a super close-up shot, while also allowing you to zoom way out to capture a panoramic view. You've already seen how zooming out on your challenge can help you gain a larger perspective on the challenges you face. But now let's try using your full zoom function to drive curiosity and deepen understanding by looking at the issues from a range of perspectives. First, try zooming in on the problem to think about it on a scale of 1:1, and imagine how the challenge impacts an individual consumer or employee. After spending some time in close range, begin to zoom out. How would the challenge be viewed by people in an entire city? Or a county or a state? How would the challenge look to a specific culture or nation? Changing your focal length from very close to very far, and every stop in between, will help increase your awareness of the situation and become more connected to possible solutions.

Tuning In

In *Tuned In*, Craig Stull, Phil Myers, and David Meerman Scott describe how the best new product ideas were discovered through the inventors' being immersed in the customer's world.[3] A classic innovation mistake is to project yourself as your target audience—just because you like grape-lime coolers doesn't mean that consumers will. The best innovations come from "tuning in" to customers. This applies to any Creativity Challenge, no matter who your "customer" may be—an internal team, a vendor, or even the boss who has to approve your idea.

The key to tuning in is empathy. The more you can understand your audience, the better you'll be able to appeal to them. Role playing is a fun way to get tuned in. Have a few people on your team act out a scene or two in the role of your customer, while the rest of your team observes and takes notes. Then switch it up and have new people act the roles. Getting close to the mind-set of the customer will help you ask better questions and ultimately produce more creative solutions.

The Outsider

A major French construction company makes new employees complete an "Astonishment Report" within thirty days after their start date. They are asked to list everything that is astonishing to them, both good and bad, about their new place of business. The rationale is that outsiders notice things that have been normalized to incumbents.

To gain a completely fresh perspective on an existing challenge, look at your processes, practices, or products like a complete outsider and ask, "Why do we do it that way?" If you just came to the situation from a different company, state, or even planet, what would you question? Having a fresh perspective can really open up your thinking—most of us don't pay much attention to the way things are in a familiar environment. For example, you probably don't pay much attention to the furniture or artwork in your house, but if you went to a new friend's house, you would probably notice those things immediately. The more you can break through familiarity, the better your creative thinking becomes.

The Periscope

Johann Gutenberg (of printing press fame) originally designed periscopes to provide the ability to see around corners as well as above the surface of obstacles. Instead of a physical periscope, imagine you have an "idea periscope." When you consider your Creativity Challenge, what information would this instrument give you? What ideas are around the corner or above the surface? If you had to guess what obstacles or fresh perspectives were outside your current line of sight, what would they be? Spend fifteen minutes on this topic with your team, and you will enjoy some really strong ideas and a boost to your awareness.

Developing the Five Skills of Master Innovators

In Chapter Two, I mentioned that studies have shown that creativity is a learned skill, rather than a "gift of nature." The December 2009 *Harvard Business Review* published the results of the most important of these studies—a comprehensive analysis of innovation titled "The Innovator's DNA." Professors from Harvard Business School, INSEAD, and Brigham Young University completed a six-year study of more than three thousand executives and five hundred innovative entrepreneurs, including such high-profile entrepreneurs as Amazon founder Jeff Bezos and Michael Dell, founder of Dell Computers. The researchers concluded that creative capacity is only 20 percent inherited, and 80 percent learned behavior—very encouraging news for those who don't feel especially creative. That's why it's important that you use the exercises in this book for building your creative muscles and expanding your creative capacity.

The researchers also concluded that these five skills separate the most accomplished innovators from the rest:

1. *Associating*. This skill involves creating links between seemingly unrelated items. The best innovators are able to connect concepts, things, and people in imaginative ways. To increase your capacity, you can increase your exposure to more and different ideas and then force yourself to think about ways in which they could be linked. Consider such connections as symphonic music with snack food, typography with travel, and catering with construction. By finding common threads and looking for similarities, overlap, or new combinations, you can unlock new forms of creativity.

2. *Questioning*. As we've already discussed, questions are at the core of creativity. In addition to asking our Three Magic Questions (Why? What if? Why not?), the best creative minds ask any number of open-ended questions. What could...? How might...? If..., then what about...? Have you thought about...? The specific content of these questions isn't as important as the process of asking and answering them. As the name of this first phase of Disciplined Dreaming suggests, Ask!

3. *Observing*. This skill involves raising your level of awareness, observing in great detail what is happening in the world, and then imagining what could be different. Scott Cook, founder of Intuit Software, the maker of Quicken, first came up with the idea for personal finance software by carefully observing his wife paying the bills and realizing all the various subtasks that consumed her time.[4] This observation set him on the path to envisioning a better way. In bringing that vision to life, his company changed the world of personal (and later corporate) financial software.

4. *Experimenting*. The most effective creative minds are not afraid of failure. Instead, they experiment and dabble until they stumble upon the best solutions. Thomas Edison generated thousands of versions of the light bulb before creating the one that changed the world.

5. *Networking*. You may think of networking as handing out business cards at a corporate mixer. In the creative process, networking is about finding diverse people whose ideas challenge your own thinking and expand your perspective. Discussing your Creativity Challenge with people who have divergent viewpoints can spark incredible insight and solutions. Seek as much diversity as possible in this network, including diversity of age, gender, political view, educational background, career role, religious perspective, and geographical location.

Avoiding the Pike Syndrome and the Brain Trap

When you find yourself stymied by invisible barriers to your creative ideas, remember the pike—a fierce and cunning carnivorous fish that eats smaller fish and always finds a way to get its prey. Scientists once conducted an experiment in which they put a pike in a tank with many smaller fish, but interfered with the expected feeding frenzy by separating the pike from its prey with a layer of glass.[5] The hungry pike continuously smashed itself against the glass, but couldn't break through the barrier. Eventually, the pike become discouraged and sank to the bottom of the tank. At that point, the scientists removed the barrier, giving the pike full access to its feast.

What happened next surprised everyone. The pike continued to ignore the smaller fish, even when they swam right next to it. The predator eventually died of starvation at the bottom of the tank, even with plenty of tasty fish easily within reach.

This phenomenon, known as the *pike syndrome,* is a great illustration of how we can become paralyzed by imaginary barriers. We may not even consider a whole set of possible solutions due to fear or some other nonexistent obstacle. The pike syndrome also can remind us that we need to respond to changes in the environment. If the pike had simply responded to change once the barrier was removed, he would have been fat and happy. Instead, he starved to death because he held on to an out-of-date assumption even when the realities of the situation had dramatically changed.

Another danger to avoid is the *brain trap.* Our brains are powerful computers, but they can sometimes lead us astray. The human brain does a fantastic job of scanning its memory and looking back at events, situations, problems, and solutions of the past. It then processes this information and quickly provides a solution based on what worked (or didn't work) before. This type of thinking helps us gain wisdom through experience and avoid making the same mistake twice.

But this type of look-back-and-solve processing can be dangerous. The very essence of creativity lies in discovering new ideas, solutions, and concepts—in an inherent conflict with how the brain likes to work. Through awareness of this trap, you can start to question the ideas that your brain suggests. Simply ask yourself, *Is this a fresh, new, and original approach, or am I simply replaying a pattern from the past?*

Raising Awareness Throughout the Organization

Remember the "Where's Waldo?" books? The fun of the books was not in the story line but in scanning the complex illustrations to find your friend in a red striped shirt hiding in the crowd.

During the process, your level of awareness skyrocketed. You noticed things you would never have noticed at first glance—the balloons in a little girl's hand, the chickens being chased by a farmer, the flower delivery man's funny pants. You were on the hunt, and you noticed just about *everything* on the page.

What would happen if you brought that same level of awareness with you to work, and specifically to your Creativity Challenge? You would notice all sorts of things that you probably skimmed right over in the past: nuances among your customers, your surroundings, and your competitors; insights into your industry, your production processes, and your sales strategy. As you use the curiosity drivers you've read about in this chapter, you'll become more aware and uncover many fresh ideas and opportunities for improvement. Some will be large opportunities that could lead to groundbreaking change, boosting both your company and your career. Others may be small improvements that when added together, also lead to meaningful results. But one of the biggest improvements you'll make in your performance will be an increased ability to *see* the information before you; you'll no longer just look at the world through bureaucratic blinders.

The costs of failing to see the information that's right in front of your nose are quite real, as I have learned from personal experience at ePrize. We had recently won a great new client, UPS. When we shipped out a packet of sales materials related to our first promotion, what did we do? We sent the materials in a brightly colored FedEx box! Just imagine the FedEx delivery person laughing as he walked into the lobby at the corporate headquarters of FedEx's biggest competitor.

As you can guess, our client didn't find the humor in this situation, and called me immediately to express her outrage. After the call, I sat down with the person at my company who sent the package and questioned her thinking. I was stunned by the lack of awareness that would allow anyone to fill out a form with a giant purple and orange FedEx logo in the corner and address it to UPS. But I was even more disappointed with my employee's response: "Our shipping contract is with FedEx."

I learned two important lessons from this experience. First, lack of awareness has a gravitational pull. It pulls people down into a state of semi-sleepwalking, in which they turn off their brains and ignore even the most obvious things in their surroundings. We as leaders need to break this gravitational pull by constantly stimulating our team members' curiosity, nurturing their natural creativity, and building their sense of awareness.

The second lesson I learned is the incredible power of rules and bureaucratic processes. People are quick to "follow along," believing it more important to obey than to do what is obviously the right thing for their company. It takes guts and creativity to question the system and take ownership of your role. But those skills are exactly what we need if we are to stand out and create sustainable advantages in today's ultracompetitive business environment. And that means we need to create a *new* culture within our organizations, one that rewards team members for questioning outdated policies. Our organizational culture should celebrate the employee who knows when it's time to buck the "standard operating procedure"—for example, by shipping packages to the UPS client via UPS instead of taking the prescribed route and sending it with a contracted carrier.

The State Bank of Mauritius is a great example of an organization that celebrates awareness and uses curiosity to win customers. The bank's officials began by questioning why interest rates are always tied to interbank transfer rates or governmental bond rates. They also had a high level of awareness and realized that their customers were crazy about football (that's "soccer" for us Americans). Wins by the region's favorite teams, Liverpool or Manchester United, would trigger street parties and tremendous excitement.

Through *curiosity* (asking *why* interest rates are tied to banking functions and *what if* they were not) and *awareness* (realizing their customers were really into football), they used *association* (linking interest rates and football) to do something really special. In a bold and creative move, the bank offered special bank accounts where customers' interest rates would vary depending on the results of their favorite teams. The bank was able to keep their profit margins intact while attracting and keeping large numbers of customers. Their curiosity, awareness, and, ultimately, creativity led to the bank standing out from competitors with a truly differentiated offering.

Mihalyi Czikszentmihalyi, professor of psychology at the University of Chicago, wrote, "Creativity generally involves crossing the boundaries of domains. The most creative among us see relationships the rest of us never notice."[6]

True originality has never emerged from a formula. Rules are precisely what innovators and other paradigm shifters break. As you work to complete step 1 of the Disciplined Dreaming process, by defining and detailing your Creativity Challenge, remember that you're building a structure that you'll use to reach new heights of creativity. The ideas and activities you've learned in this chapter—drivers of an unbridled sense of curiosity and awareness— are your building blocks for that process.

Building Your Creativity Chops

This chapter has offered a number of great ideas for driving curiosity and expanding awareness as you and your team form a clear vision of your Creativity Challenge. Here are some quick ways that you and your team can expand on those ideas:

1. **What are your meatloaves?** Gather a small team of people (no more than could be fed by two pizzas) and list the embedded processes in your organization. Discuss openly

why these rules are in place and whether the reasons that first made them necessary still exist.

2. **Find the fix-ups.** To build awareness, set a timer for three minutes and write down everything you can see in the room around you that could be improved. The small chip of paint in the lower left corner of the room. The sloppy cords around the projector. The painting that is tilted slightly to the right. The one out of eight fluorescent bulbs that is missing from the light fixture. The small coffee stain on your chair. This quick exercise is a great warm-up for brainstorming sessions. It works well both individually and for teams.

3. **Name it!** You and your team have just been hired as creative directors at OPI, and your first job is to invent names for new OPI colors. Take five minutes and brainstorm a list of new names for nail polish. Make sure the names are fun, suggestive, mysterious, adventuresome, alluring, or some combination of these.

4. **Act like a six-year-old.** Six-year-olds tend to overflow with curiosity and question everything. Six-year-olds tell it like it is. They love to pretend, and their imaginations are almost limitless. You can't act like a six-year-old all the time—you have to lead your company, be a parent, and pay the bills. But schedule a two-hour block every week or so and use it to put yourself back in a six-year-old mind-set. If you have a six-year-old child, even better. Take some time to play on a six-year-old's terms, and see if you don't learn a thing or two about how she approaches her surroundings and how she is fueled by her curiosity and imagination.

5. **Flood the house to catch the mouse.** Use a brainstorming session to invent a better mousetrap. Begin by questioning

and challenging everything. Why does a mousetrap need to use a spring? What other ways are there to catch a mouse? How could a mouse be contained in a completely different way? The more radical your breakthrough thinking and ideas, the better—for example, "What if we filled the entire house with water in order to flood the mice out?" No, you wouldn't flood a house to kill a mouse, but perhaps you'd invent a mousetrap that catches mice in a water-based trap. The goal is to push yourself and your team outside normal boundaries and let your imaginations run wild. You can always reel them back in when you need to.

PREPARE

5

Gaining the Keys to a Creative Mind and Culture

Our culture is what gives us the best chance of continuous success for many generations of technology and people.

—REED HASTINGS, FOUNDER AND CHAIRMAN, NETFLIX

It was 4 P.M. on a Thursday afternoon, when the ePrize phones went dead, the servers shut down, and e-mail and BlackBerry usage stopped cold. My staff was confused and about to hit the panic button.

Then came the announcement: "I am kidnapping the company," I said in a serious tone. We hustled everyone outside and told the group to meet immediately at the closest Best Buy store. Upon arrival, I gave everyone a $200 gift card along with a specific instruction: "Here's a little bonus. You are not allowed to save it. You have to spend it RIGHT NOW."

The store erupted in pandemonium, with over three hundred people running down the aisles. Team members compared notes while passing each other in the aisles. An Xbox or that hot new digital camera? A new printer or a portable XM radio? The poor store manager and cashiers were overwhelmed as our giddy team shopped, laughed, joked, and had an all-around great time.

Two years later, team members still beam about the experience. Besides the monetary reward, the experience reinforced that they worked for a fun, creative company that loved to do things differently. If we issued everyone a $200 bonus that showed up in his or her regular paycheck, that money would be largely overlooked and quickly forgotten. Instead, we created a memorable experience—doing something unique and fun that was representative not just of the work we do but of who we are as individuals and as members of the ePrize culture. This experience was just one of the ways that we at ePrize work to build a creative culture and to help keep each of our team members mentally prepared for exercising his or her unique creative capacity.

Creativity demands preparation. When Yo Yo Ma, one of the world's most accomplished cellists, is scheduled to perform a featured solo for a sold-out audience at Carnegie Hall, he intensely prepares for the concert. He arrives early to tune his cello, checks in with the conductor, makes sure his tuxedo is in order, and tests the acoustics of the performance hall. He establishes a solid working relationship with his accompanying musicians and business colleagues, so that they all work in harmony (excuse the pun) to support his larger creative vision.

We know that top performers in every field go through similar types of preparation, from surgeons to space shuttle pilots to computer chip manufacturers. Why then is the concept of preparation to enable creativity neglected in the business world? The budget for landscaping at most companies geometrically outweighs the investment in creativity preparation, yet fresh thinking and new ideas are infinitely more important than well-trimmed shrubbery.

Step 2 of the Disciplined Dreaming process is all about preparation—you use this step to make sure that you are mentally poised for creativity and that you will be tackling the creative process in a culture and environment that promote your greatest creative capacity. In this chapter, we will talk about preparing your mind and culture; in Chapter Six, we explore ideas for creating a physical environment that sparks ideas and breeds creativity and innovation.

Preparing Your Mind for the Creative Process

You need to be in the right frame of mind to free yourself from creative barriers and release your true creative potential. The right mental state can make the difference between breakthrough and blasé. In addition, the right focus and mind-set will provide you with fulfillment and joy as they serve as a foundation for your creative expression.

Like Yo Yo Ma, many people at the top of their game have specific warm-up rituals that prepare them for optimal performance. Tony Robbins, the world-famous motivational speaker, jumps on a portable trampoline for three to five minutes before every speech. Lennox Lewis, the former heavyweight boxing champion, listened to fast, intense jazz music on a headset before every fight. In the same way that a musician warms up her fingers with scales and stretching exercises before giving a concert, you can warm up your mind and get in the zone. Preparing yourself to be creative will allow you to unleash your best ideas right out of the gate.

Warming Up: The Top Ten Moves

As with any challenge, the creative process is more effective after a good warm-up. Some simple activities and games can prime your creative pump and get your brain firing. The specific exercises you use to warm up are far less important than the act of going through the warm-up itself. I encourage you to create your own "mental gymnastics" for yourself and your team, but here are my top ten creativity warm-up moves:

1.   **The beach ball.** Bring a beach ball to your next meeting and toss it around for ninety seconds before you get to work. You'll be amazed at how the energy changes in the room and how this simple physical act can get the creative juices flowing.

2.   **Rock the house.** Blast three minutes of your favorite music. *Loud*. As a fun alternative, ask each person in the room to suggest a favorite song, then combine thirty-second cuts of each song into a quick playlist. You and your team will be pumped up and ready to create.

3.   **The deep breath.** Have everyone close his or her eyes and do two minutes of deep breathing. After that, do two minutes of random stretching. The blood will be flowing, just like the creative ideas you are about to generate.

4.   **The improv.** One person starts and says a few words or a sentence. The next person has to continue the story where the first person left off. The one rule: you can never say "No" to someone's previous statement, only "Yes, and" and build from there. Continue for three to five minutes or until your whole group is flat on the floor with laughter.

5.   **The field trip.** Get out of the office! Go to a museum, park, coffee shop, or anywhere else that is inspiring and outside the norm.

6.   **Games.** Play a game (any game) for five minutes. A board game, riddle, puzzle, card game, even Xbox. Games get you in a different state of mind, helping you escape the daily grind and open up your imagination.

7.   **Practice round.** Before attacking your actual Creativity Challenge, do a practice round of mental exploration. For example,

ask, "What are five ways we could reduce crime in our city?" Ask a broad and unusual question that has nothing to do with your company, and let the team have fun with it.

8. **Draw your neighbor.** Sit in a circle and have everyone sketch the person to his or her right, without labeling the drawings. (Do right instead of left because people will subconsciously be using the right, creative side of their brains.) Give a five-minute time limit. Tape the sketches to a wall and see if people can guess who's who.

9. **The magazine story.** Take a magazine and flip to any random photograph. Ask the person to your right to tell a story about that picture in great detail using characters and emotion. Pass the magazine to the next person, pick a new picture, and repeat. By the time you go around the room, the team's imagination will be on point.

10. **Inspirational quotes.** Print a list of relevant quotes (find dozens at www.CreativityGeneration.com), go around the room, and have each person read one quote slowly and out loud. After reading all quotes, reflect on them. Have each person tell the group which was his or her favorite quote and why.

Although these activities are great warm-ups, they also are very helpful during the creative process. Use liberally between creative bursts (every forty-five to ninety minutes) to respark your team's energy and continue to generate the best possible ideas. (You'll find a few additional warm-up ideas, along with some important creativity myths and truths, in the appendix to this book.)

Recognizing Creativity Killers

Like rush-hour traffic in Los Angeles, your creative ability can come to a screeching halt if the road is blocked. That's why it is important to understand the key blockers of creativity so that you can avoid the gridlock and get on with creating your own art, whatever the medium may happen to be. I've mentioned the creativity-killing effect of fear, the status quo, and a rigid adherence to obedience. Here are some other common killers of creativity that can invade our mental space. Be on the lookout and ready to banish them the moment they appear.

Groupthink Everyone likes agreement: it feels nice when a group of people are all aligned and everyone has the chance to contribute. But "getting along" can destroy your creative potency. I call this killer *groupthink*—a term you've probably heard before, but used in a slightly different context. Allowing the groupthink creativity killer to invade your mental process can dilute the power of an idea by burying the creative spark under a flood of disjointed ideas.

Imagine, for example, that you and your team are working to develop a new flavor of ice cream. One person says, "How about pink grapefruit flavor?" The next person adds, "You know what would really make that special—a slight taste of basil added to it." Now if you stopped right there, you could have something fantastic, compelling, and new. Unfortunately, business brainstorming sessions rarely stop there. It's true that while you're in the creative process, the more ideas the better. But you have to be prepared to draw a single, winning idea from all of that input. Too often, weak leaders attempt to mush together every idea in an effort to pacify the team and create "buy-in." As a result of this kind of groupthink, what started as a powerful idea can end up a jumbled, ineffective mess.

Groupthink can also crush ideas in reverse, by dragging what should be something remarkable into yet another me-too plan. Ben and Jerry could have been easily convinced by their team that each new flavor was too radical or that one ingredient or another creates too much risk. Has your company ever had a great idea (the business equivalent of Cherry Garcia) that got overanalyzed and ended up as pure vanilla? Whichever form it takes, make sure that groupthink isn't diluting your creative process. Refer back to your "Where's Waldo?" awareness to determine when great ideas start to get mucked up and lose their potency. A good litmus test is to ask yourself, Has this idea become more compelling and remarkable, or has it become either too complicated (driven by consensus building) or too watered down (driven by fear)?

The Whac-A-Mole You remember this game: furry animals shoot up from holes in a table, and as you whack one down, another pops up. Solving creative challenges can be a similar experience—solve one, and another crops up to take its place. The whole cycle can be confusing and frustrating, and can ultimately derail your creative process.

Avoid becoming distracted: stick to one Creativity Challenge at a time, and then keep a running list of new issues that pop up. I call this list a Parking Lot. You can go back to the Parking Lot when you've finished dealing with the challenge at hand.

The Missing Mojo You need mojo for the creative process, even though it exists only in your mind: if you believe you have it, you do. At the same time, if you think you've lost it, you have. Mojo has little do to with skill, intelligence, experience, or artistic ability; it's all about confidence and attitude. One easy way to overcome a lack of mojo is to close your eyes and spend two or three minutes thinking you are someone else—Mick Jagger, Jackson Pollock, or Beethoven—and imagining what it would feel like to be that person (what you ate for breakfast, what your bedroom looks like, your agenda for the day). After a few deep breaths, open your eyes and boldly state out loud, "I'm Mick Jagger" (or whomever else you chose). Now go to work on your Creativity Challenge, bringing all of that person's swagger and certainty to the job. Your creativity will skyrocket along with your mojo.

The Identity Crisis When you wear more than one hat during the creative process, creativity hits a brick wall. It goes something like this. You are in the middle of coming up with a great idea and acting the role of creator, writing a sentence or drawing a diagram on the whiteboard. Suddenly, your brain flips, and you take on a different role. You become an editor, and your mind becomes focused on potential mistakes: "Should this be slide four, or slide nine?" "Did I misspell *cross-functional*?" Or you begin to worry about how you'll implement your idea, and the voice of the executor pops up in your mind: "How am I ever going to get the funding for this?" "Will Bob in HR approve my request?" "When will I fit this into the schedule?" "If I get this done, will I get a raise?"

> *You cannot simultaneously prevent and prepare for war.*
>
> —ALBERT EINSTEIN

Editing and executing are left-brain activities, using the part of your brain that manages analytical, practical, and formulaic thinking. The creative act is driven by your right brain, the area reserved for abstract thought and imagination. We live in a predominantly left-brain world, so your left brain is probably much more developed than your right brain. That means your left brain can quickly take over and dominate your thinking, in the same way that a loudmouth bragger can take over and dominate a conversation at a cocktail party. In the process, your creative spark gets lost, and your creativity is hampered.

If you are worried about making everything perfect before you go to the next step, you will end up *executing* your best thinking all right, but not in a good way. So when you and your team are in the creative mode, be there fully. Force yourself to let your creative voice hold the floor, and tell the editor and executor to shut up.

You can avoid left-brain takeover by drawing attention to its first signs. Bring a small bell to your next creative meeting, and anytime someone starts getting into editor or executor mode, ring the bell. By putting a little reverse Pavlov to use, you'll be breaking the habit of distraction and driving the creativity executioner from your mind. Your creativity will come to life.

Building Creative Cultures

Mental preparation is a good place to start getting ready for the creative process, but a creative mind needs a creative culture in which to flourish. There is an undeniable correlation in organizations between high levels of innovation and cultures that nurture creativity. Although in the past these environments were looked down on as being "soft," nowadays establishing a corporate culture that enables team members to express their creativity is fundamentally linked to business success.

Getting it right is not an easy thing, especially in an organization that has deeply entrenched, old-school values. In the Industrial Age, businesses won by extracting the most manual labor out of workers; in the Information Age, the most precision and efficiency. In today's Age of Creativity, your key challenge is to unleash creative ideas from your team in order to drive meaningful business performance. That makes building a creative culture one of your primary jobs as a leader in the new era of business.

Establishing—and Living—Core Values

At ePrize, we built just such a culture. Our team was so passionate and connected that we were able to beat the odds, change an industry, and enjoy tremendous success. Our creative culture helped drive performance across the business, in hiring, retention, job satisfaction, client satisfaction, product development, sales performance, brand building, and even production efficiencies.

One mantra was "*Who* we are is more important than *what* we do." What we do will continue to change as the industry, technology, market conditions, and competitors evolve. Who we are—our core values and the way we live our business lives—is our foundation, and doesn't fluctuate with market trends. Our core values are nonnegotiable, and serve as an important benchmark for our behavior and decision making.

We started by clearly articulating our core values and sharing them continuously with our team, vendors, clients, investors, and anyone else who would listen. We put a theme around them: *the Power of "e"*—the highest level of performance. We don't provide great customer service; we provide great customer service to the power of "e"! We don't innovate new products; we do that to the power of "e." Our Power of "e" culture has ten core values:

1. Passion^e
2. Trust^e
3. Creativity^e
4. Innovation^e
5. Higher thinking^e
6. Communication^e
7. Collaboration^e
8. Results^e
9. Evolution^e
10. Extraordinary^e

Each month, I spend up to four hours with new employees—"newPrizers." I don't talk to them about their jobs, our clients, or what we do. Instead, I focus only on who we are. I walk them through stories and examples, and discuss each value in detail. It's important for me to ensure that they understand our culture and how highly we value it.

A welcome session isn't enough to reinforce the values to the point where people live and breathe them, so we wrote a short book about our culture (free download at www.CreativityGeneration .com), hold regular company meetings about culture, give awards and prizes to people who have lived our values, and focus on these cultural values as a major part of team members' performance evaluations. Merely saying you support creativity won't shape a creative culture. Identify the core values that make you and your organization a breeding ground for creativity and then express those values in everything you do.

Celebrating Creativity and Connectedness

Building a creative culture is a process that can be an adventure in itself. In addition to living its core values, for example, Zappos does some other really cool things to build a culture of creativity:[1]

- It has a full-time life coach available at anytime for any team member.
- It puts out an annual yearbook in which team members reflect on the culture. Everything is published, good or bad, in any format—poems, songs, drawings, stories, and so on.
- After a two-week training program, the company offers new employees a $2,000 bonus to quit. No questions asked. If people decide to stay, Zappos knows they are the right cultural fit.
- The company has a free library and educational program to help team members learn and grow, even on topics unrelated to their jobs.

How Quicken Loans and Zappos Set the Bar

Clearly articulating values and then truly living them are hallmarks of success for the most creative next-generation companies. Quicken Loans, the largest online mortgage company with over $25 billion in annual mortgage originations, is passionate about its creative culture and spends a lot of time and money instilling core values throughout its three-thousand-person organization. Some of those values include[2]

- Remaining obsessed with finding a better way.
- We are the "they."
- A sense of urgency is the ante to play.
- A penny saved is a penny.
- You have to take the roast out of the oven.

Tony Hsieh, CEO of Zappos, credits the company's creative culture as its most important competitive advantage. Zappos invests heavily in its culture, which is built around these specific core values:

- Deliver WOW through service
- Embrace and drive change
- Create fun and a little weirdness
- Be adventurous, creative, and open minded
- Pursue growth and learning
- Build open and honest relationships with communication
- Build a positive team and family spirit
- Do more with less
- Be passionate and determined
- Be humble

In addition to our Power of "e" sessions, here are a few other things that we at ePrize have done to build a culture specifically designed to nurture and develop creativity:

- **Staff call.** Each month, we have a full-company huddle in which we, as a team, share our successes, take our challenges head-on, have fun, and express ourselves. Part corporate communication, part pep rally, these sessions have become very theatrical and hilarious. As a company, we've laughed through raps, comedy bits, practical jokes, and improv skits. These events celebrate creativity, connection, and personal expression.

- **eeek-Prize.** Every Halloween, we transform our headquarters into a haunted house, and the entire team dresses up in elaborate costumes to compete for prizes. We hold an open Halloween bash and invite all team members to bring in their kids and those of their friends, family, and neighbors. One year we had more than eight hundred kids in the building—trick-or-treating, bobbing for apples, playing games, going through the eeek-Prize haunted house, dancing to scary music, making balloon animals, and generally having a blast. Besides the pure joy of watching kids have a great time, this is a unifying event for our team that stirs passion and creativity and promotes team satisfaction.

- **Annual themes.** It started with the Year of the Client—a Chinese dragon theme that served as a rallying cry for our team around the importance of delighting our clients. We rolled out the theme with food, decorations, music, and fun. Since that time, the rollouts for our annual themes have become increasingly dramatic. Our 2006 theme, No Limits, had all the leaders of the company dressed up as superheroes (capes and all), as we danced to the music of *The Incredibles,* staged fake fight scenes, and basically made total jerks of ourselves. Annual themes have been a strong technique for energizing the team and fostering creativity.

- **Practical jokes.** A team member who came back from a week's vacation returned to his desk perfectly in order—but now located on the roof of our building. On one random Tuesday, about thirty people dressed up as our chief operating officer and acted the part for the entire day. Well-chosen pranks (with objects who can take it) can create a culture of fun in which people feel comfortable expressing themselves.

Remembering Who You *Aren't*

You can also increase creativity and forge connectedness by remembering what your culture *isn't*. To put a glaring light on the types of attitudes and approaches that divide team members and stifle their creativity, we at ePrize, along with our friends at Quicken Loans, created these characters and their "backstories." Meet the Promo-Shuns—a motley crew of bad dudes who are the enemy—the antithesis of our culture:

Lola Vel. Lola is easily distracted. Head in the clouds, she has a very low level of awareness. She lacks urgency and can't focus on what is truly important. Because she's so unaware, she can't ever seem to generate any creativity.

Lola Vel

Dee Fensiv. It's tough to talk with Dee, because she always feels attacked. She is so insecure and lacking in trust, she can't have a rational discussion. She avoids constructive conflict, so she can't be "blamed" for anything. Don't look for innovation here—she's scared of her own shadow.

Dee Fensiv

Luke Atme. Luke is a "spectacle maker." He always calls attention to himself and wants everyone to know how smart he is and what's going on with *him*. This discourages collaboration, depletes his fellow teammates, and trips up his ability to make a difference.

Luke Atme

Nora Sponse. Talking to Nora is like talking to a wall. Don't expect a response! She moves slowly and would rather gossip than get anything done. She hates having to answer to anyone...even herself.

Nora Sponse

Lou Polle. Lou skates through the day and always takes the easy way out. He cuts corners and finds ways to work the system rather than improve it. He can't be trusted and is a big excuse maker. He attacks clarity as he hides in red tape and cop-outs.

Lou Polle

Vic and Tim. Twins Vic and Tim wish they had even more fingers to point at others. Everything in life happens *to* them. They can't be held accountable—it's always everyone else's fault. They'd rather tell you their tales of woe than be part of the solution.

Vic and Tim

- **Surprise and delight.** We are always trying to do little things that fire up our team. There have been days where our executive team shows up early, puts on aprons, and cooks breakfast for the whole company. We've hosted tailgate parties, barbeques, hot dog eating contests, and happy hours. An ePrize rock band performs regularly at company events. We offer free yoga, free martial arts, lunch-n-learn sessions from outside speakers, and even manicures. These little perks create a culture in which people love their job and their company, and care deeply about our collective success.

These are just some of the ways that cultures like those at ePrize, Quicken Loans, and Zappos not only attract the most creative and talented people but also become fertile ecosystems of ideas. Open, fun, and creative cultures allow team members to express themselves and leave their fingerprints on the organization. In turn, the companies benefit from breakthrough innovation, happy customers, low attrition, and (believe it or not) a significantly better bottom line.

Following the Seven Rules of Creative Cultures

Every great structure requires ongoing maintenance. You can keep your creative culture alive and flourishing by making sure your operation is guided by these seven critical rules:

1. Fuel passion
2. Celebrate ideas
3. Foster autonomy
4. Encourage courage
5. Fail forward
6. Think small
7. Maximize diversity

Let's take a detailed look at each of these important rules.

Fueling Passion

> *The most powerful weapon on earth is the human soul on fire.*
>
> —FERDINAND FOCH

Every great invention, every medical breakthrough, every advance of humankind began with passion: a passion for change, for making the world a better place, for contributing, for making a difference. With a team full of passion, you can accomplish just about anything. Without passion, your employees become mere clock-punching automatons. Here are some powerful ways to promote passion in your team:

- **Develop a sense of purpose.** Companies that can rally their teams around a clear and important purpose inject passion deep into their teams. Steve Jobs wanted to "put a ding in the universe." Whole Foods Market wanted to be the world's leading natural and organic foods supermarket retailer. BMW set out to create the Ultimate Driving Machine. Your purpose needn't be corporate, but it should be about big, important ideas. You may run a nonprofit organization whose purpose is to help boost educational standards in inner cities, or you might be a politician determined to enact reform on behalf of your constituents. Your purpose has to answer the question, "Besides the paycheck, why am I coming to work every day?" The better that answer is, the more passion you will evoke.

- **Promote collaboration.** Working with a team and getting pumped up from the collective energy of the group is a potent source of passion. When motivated people work together, a $1 + 1 = 3$ effect occurs. Human connections are also important to help work through the inevitable setbacks or challenges. And passion is contagious.

- **Have fun.** Having fun puts you in the zone and optimizes your brain chemistry for creativity. British Airways now employs a full-time "corporate jester." Google has sand volleyball courts on its corporate campus to seamlessly connect "work" and "fun." Companies like Zest Corporate Adventures exist to build teamwork and creativity not through doing more work but by having more fun. Fun promotes passion by opening your team up to fresh possibilities, elevating their energy and enthusiasm, and encouraging them to approach even the most challenging problems with a fresh perspective.

Celebrating Ideas

You can learn more about a person in an hour of play than in a year of conversation.

—PLATO

The Israeli company Iscar makes metalworking cutting tools, but more important, it is driven by innovation. The company pioneered technology advances in its industry, from products to manufacturing to distribution. Iscar's culture cherishes creativity and rewards the best ideas at all times. Its corporate campus is understated—no giant logos, no fancy buildings; there's just one visible sign stretched across the top of one very long building. In gigantic letters, the sign reads: WHERE INNOVATION NEVER STOPS. Warren Buffett sees the value in Iscar's creative culture: in 2006, Berkshire Hathaway purchased 80 percent of Iscar for $4 billion.

Cultures of all kinds form around social norms—those that are celebrated and those that are punished. Many businesses give lip service to their celebration of innovation, but punish, rather

Playforce

As kids, we go out to play. Later in life, we play sports or play music, but we adults leave our homes each day and go to *work*. The term implies doing something uninspired, often boring.

What if we flipped the terminology and substituted "play" for "work"? In place of a workforce, our companies could have a playforce. "Bye, honey, I'm running off to play." "Oh great, dear; have a nice day at the playground." Have a conflict? Maybe you should "play" it out.

Play stimulates the mind and the soul, and allows us to break out of the drudgery. Work is about completing tasks, maximizing efficiency, and delivering outcomes. Play can do those things too, but we add fun, imagination, movement, and an energizing lightheartedness to the mix.

Even if you can't force a company-wide change in terminology, go ahead and make the swap in your own mind. You'll notice a new bounce in your step and a renewed sense of energy and excitement about the day ahead. Forget about working through your next tough business challenge... try playing through it instead.

than reward, risk-taking and creativity. In a creative culture, rewards come in many forms: money, yes, but great businesses also celebrate creativity through praise (both public and private), career opportunities, and perks. If you want your team to be creative, you need to establish an environment that celebrates and rewards them accordingly.

Fostering Autonomy Creativity is an act of self-expression. People and teams that can call their own shots are better able to produce valuable creative output, whereas a person who has to run every minute detail by her boss for approval will quickly become numb to the creative process. That's why fostering autonomy is a critical step in maintaining a creative culture.

Randall Dunn, the head of the innovative Roeper School, works to maintain a culture that supports autonomy. "I give my

The Idea Challenge

How are you celebrating the best ideas in your company? One new trend that many companies have adopted is the Idea Challenge. At Nike, for example, a leader may invite a department (or the entire company) to see who can come up with the best idea for a new nonslip jogging shoe sole, and offer prizes and recognition for the winning idea. Broad-based Idea Challenges are very powerful for several reasons: (1) they engage a wide, diverse audience; (2) they get everyone in the team or company thinking critically about a company challenge; (3) they signify that great ideas come from everywhere in the organization; and (4) they send a clear signal that the company celebrates creativity. Industries that have issued Idea Challenges report benefits far beyond the great ideas they initially generate. Teams who participate feel capable and empowered, and many demonstrate increased overall creativity.

team lots of freedom to make their own decisions, and support their passion and creativity. I collaborate with them instead of boss them around. I really make sure people feel listened to. I have to let people feel empowered, and celebrate nonconventional thinking. Our institution wins as a result of extending trust."[3]

Dunn has it right: granting autonomy does require extending trust. Your team may make decisions differently than you do—that's what creativity is all about. The key is to provide a clear message of what results you are looking for or what problem you want the team to solve—and then to get out of the way and let them do their best work. By showing your team that you are behind them and value their judgment and creativity, you can end up with both the results you were seeking and a highly motivated and more confident team.

Encouraging Courage Netflix is known as much for its creative culture as its innovative business model. The company has continued to grow and thrive by encouraging employees to take creative risks without fear. They tell their employees to "Say what you think, even if it is controversial. Make tough decisions without excessive agonizing. Take smart risks. Question actions inconsistent with our values."[4]

John Balardo, the CEO and publisher of Hour Media, which produces *dBusiness, HOUR Detroit, Detroit Home*, and several other high-quality lifestyle and business magazines, has built a culture that empowers his team to take risks and express themselves with courage. "I created the culture to be loose . . . to allow people the freedom to explore their ideas. I allow people the opportunity to fail, and they end up succeeding. All I would have is 'plain vanilla' if I hovered over people. That hovering would squash creativity. Instead, I encourage my team to let their ideas flow freely. I try to create a *beehive of creativity*."[5]

Failing Forward In most companies, people are so afraid of making mistakes that they don't pursue success. But simply following the rules and keeping their heads down prevents them from realizing their full potential. As a business leader, you need to be very tolerant of risk-taking and setbacks. Rather than thinking of something that doesn't work immediately as a "failure," think about it as an experiment. I call these experiments Failing Forward, because each one leads you one step closer to the perfect solution.

James Dyson, the inventor of the Dyson vacuum cleaner, "failed" at over five thousand prototypes before getting it just right.[6] In fact, nearly every breakthrough innovation in history came after countless setbacks, mistakes, and "failures." When you study the great innovators and achievers, you find that they weren't necessarily smarter or inherently more talented. They simply kept trying. They didn't let setbacks or misfires extinguish their curiosity and imagination.

Becoming Your Own Worst Enemy: Slither

In 2005, ePrize had become the dominant player in the prizes and promotions industry, organizing sweepstakes, loyalty programs, and prize games for clients like Coca-Cola, Disney, General Mills, Dell, and Citibank. Like any market leader, we needed to keep our edge and avoid complacency, but, for the moment, things looked rosy indeed.

And then something happened that confirmed our worst fears. A new company entered the promotions business and threatened our market position. Every time we tried to land a new client, our rivals won the business by underpricing us and being better salespeople. They seemed to have come up with a secret way of doing our bread-and-butter work at lower cost yet with higher efficiency. Soon they were bigger than we were, and they moved faster, and—though I hated to admit it—they seemed smarter as well as a lot luckier. It seemed inevitable: Slither was going to eat our lunch unless we upped our game and out-Slithered Slither.

But here's the thing. The Slither Corporation doesn't actually exist. It's our fictive nemesis, our imaginary bad guys. Rather than battling a poorly performing company, we went up against our worst enemy—the company that *we knew* could put us out of business (if it really existed).

Slither, complete with corporate logo, became a key part of our culture. We intercepted internal memos from Slither that gave us insight into their strategy. We asked team members such questions as, "What's the one thing that your counterpart at Slither does better than you?" The team didn't have to worry about offending a colleague—if they said the wrong thing, so what? It was Slither answering, not Sally from finance. Slither even invaded our company one day, dressed in costumes that represented the opposite of our cultural values.

Inventing an ideal imaginary competitor can be a powerful way to prepare yourself and your team for maximum creative impact. In addition to creating tremendous urgency (Slither never has a down quarter), it can help break through creative barriers and prepare your imagination to shine. A made-up enemy is not only a lot of fun but can be a powerful tool to ignite free thinking.

Rather than shunning failure, many organizations encourage it:

- A medical devices company in Germany issues a Failure of the Year award at its annual company award ceremony, to encourage employees to unleash their creativity, even if the end result isn't ideal.

- A software company in Boston gives each team member two "I Screwed Up cards" every year. The equivalent of a corporate Get out of Jail Free pass, the cards allow the holder to take risks and suffer no repercussions for mistakes.

- A math professor at a top university bases 10 percent of each student's grade on making mistakes. He believes that math (yes, math!) is a creative discipline that requires new and innovative ways of solving problems, so he demands that his students try new things. If they play it safe and just follow the rules, their grades go down.

Failing Forward is about taking risks and increasing the rate of experimentation, knowing full well that some experiments won't pan out. The key is to fail quickly. Flush out ideas and let go of the ones that fail.

Thinking Small When you want your creative culture to foster big ideas, it's important to think small. Smaller companies tend to be more curious and nimble. They have a stronger sense of urgency and are not afraid to embrace change. In contrast, larger organizations often exist to protect old ideas rather than to create new ones. Research by the Doblin Group found that 96 percent of innovation resources at large companies are focused on incremental innovation.[7] Although improvements to existing business efforts are important, it is not surprising that entrepreneurial upstarts, not their big, clunky counterparts, are often the ones that create breakthrough innovation.

Here are some other ways that small and large companies differ:

Small Company	Big Company
Embraces risk	Is risk-averse
Urgency	Lethargy
Fast moving	Slow
Creates new ideas	Protects old ideas
Idea-centric	Rule-centric
Bottom-up	Top-down
Nimble	Bureaucratic
Fire in the belly	Complacent

Of course, you aren't necessarily doomed if you work in a large company. ITW is a diversified manufacturing company that produces a wide array of products, from industrial packaging to food equipment. Although it's a $16 billion company that's nearly one hundred years old, ITW thinks small. Its leaders believe that being nimble, hungry, and entrepreneurial is the key to business success. Like an amoeba, any time a business unit reaches $200 million in revenue, the unit divides into two $100 million units. ITW would rather have ten independently run and innovative $100 million units than a single bureaucratic and behemoth $1 billion unit.

Even though you may not be able to bring about this kind of massive, company-wide change, you can most likely create a ton of impact within your team by encouraging it to think like its own small, entrepreneurial company and by remaining nimble, innovative, and creative.

Maximizing Diversity Ziba, a top innovation consulting firm in Portland, Oregon, is known for its diverse workforce—120 employees of eighteen different nationalities who together speak a total of twenty-six languages. The company also has an "ambassador program" that has employees spend three months working in other disciplines (known as "tribes") within the organization. During that time, the ambassador team member really participates as part of those teams. "This helps to create an understanding of another world," says Sohrab Vossoughi, the firm's founder and president. That diversity of thought and perspective, in turn, fuels creativity. It also translates to business results: Ziba is one of the most prolific and successful innovation firms in the world.[8]

Diversity in all its shapes, colors, and flavors helps build creative cultures. As big as the world has become, individuals still make individual purchase decisions. As competition increases, generic one-size-fits-all products and services are easily supplanted by products tailored to niche audiences. To connect with customers, you need to really understand the world from their perspective, not yours—this is one area where a diverse culture can make a huge difference.

Connecting Your Culture to the Future

Once an organization loses its spirit of pioneering and rests on its early work, its progress stops.

—THOMAS WATSON, FORMER CEO OF IBM

When it comes to innovation, organizations can become disabled by experience and specialization. Large companies are typically structured by department, resulting in incremental improvements rather than holistic innovation.

To compete in the Age of Creativity, companies large or small need to act more like entrepreneurial start-ups. Young companies are more likely to invent the future. In addition to having more passion and urgency, they have little respect for tradition

At Pixar, Creativity Is King

Ed Catmull, the founder and CEO of Pixar Animation Studios, ties Pixar's success directly to its culture and the company's ability to nurture and develop creativity. Pixar executives have never bought a script; every one of the studio's amazing creative breakthroughs was developed internally.[9]

Three core principles are critical to Pixar's success:

- Anyone must have the freedom to communicate with anyone.
- It must be safe for everyone to offer ideas.
- We must stay close to innovations in the academic community.

Pixar has a group called the Brain Trust, consisting of eight directors. As each of these people works on his or her own projects, any one of them can bring a creative problem to the Brain Trust for a two-hour give-and-take session. This is a format with no ego. The group dynamics are based on trust and respect. The Brain Trust has no authority; final decisions for each movie are still left to one director. Participants feel comfortable giving and receiving straight-between-the-eyes advice, and the collaborative environment enables the best creative ideas to surface.

Another practical tool Pixar uses is called the Daily; each day, teams hold review and feedback sessions on works in progress (unlike other studios, where people work alone or in silos and share work as a final product). The Daily fosters collaborative creativity and allows many people to offer ideas and insight as the creative work is being developed. Head director John Lasseter credits the Daily with helping the studio develop better work in a more streamlined manner. Even the Pixar building contributes to creative collaboration, its central atrium fostering random encounters between staff.

Catmull sums up Pixar's approach to creativity this way: "Our secret was that we used a set of principles and practices for managing creativity. We focused on building a sustainable creative organization, using values and culture to get there. If you want to be original, you have to accept the uncertainty, even when it's uncomfortable, and have the capacity to recover when your organization takes a big risk and fails."[10]

and are not restrained by history, preconceptions, or previous failures.

At Silk Route Global, a high-growth international logistics company, the team is focused on staying nimble and finding new ideas. CEO Amjad Hussain literally threw away the org chart. "In our 80-person company, no one reports to anyone else. There are no bosses. Everyone has a mentor instead of a boss, and people serve each other in that capacity. We all know what we have to do and are very clear on our company objectives. I decided to do away with hierarchy altogether and provide freedom and ownership in order to get more done."[11]

As you build your own creative culture, focus on empowering your team to reach its highest potential. Like the leader of a jazz combo, you need to give everyone a solo—a chance to shine in the spotlight and take joy in pushing his or her creativity to the limit. By encouraging responsible risk-taking, you create a culture that gives team members the freedom and autonomy to unlock their creativity without the fear of failure.

Building Your Creativity Chops

To prepare your mind and culture for maximum creative output, here are just a few more ideas and activities you and your team can use to prepare for tackling Creativity Challenges—and have a bit of fun in the process:

1. **Issue an Idea Challenge.** You can extend the challenge to your team, department, or whole company. Set a modest prize, detail the recognition and nontangible rewards the winners will receive (anything from money to special parking), identify the Creativity Challenge behind this contest, and don't forget to include a deadline and the format in which you'd like the responses (five hundred words or less, for example). Even leaders who are reluctant at first to try this

become fast converts as they see the tangible and emotional benefits it produces.

2. **Push your team to "fail."** Issue an assignment to see who can come up with the most outrageous idea (instead of the safest). By pushing your team to Fail Forward, you can unleash creative capacity that you didn't even know existed.

6

●

Preparing Your Environment to Promote Creative Passion

If I had eight hours to chop down a tree, I'd spend six hours sharpening my axe.

—ABRAHAM LINCOLN

Eva Niewiadomski discovered something special while working as a marketing executive at Quaker Oats, a division of PepsiCo. In the early days of her career, she decided to decorate her cubicle with fun colors, toys, and images. She wanted to have a creative workspace. When she was promoted and received her own office, she decorated the office with the same playful creativity. Vibrant colors, rich textures, games, toys, and art supplies became her trademark. When she was away on business trips, others would sneak in to her office to check out what a cool, creative space Eva had created.[1]

Eva took over an unused wall in her department and transformed it into a wall of competitive insight—for example, by using it to display a striking and visceral collage comparing Quaker's product packaging with its competitors'. As Eva's career progressed inside Quaker, she continued to create inspiring spaces with every move and promotion, and she saw the impact these spaces had on people's creativity. By being surrounded with colors and fun, she and her colleagues had better ideas. This insight led her to leave

109

her job and launch one of the coolest businesses I've seen: Catalyst Ranch (www.CatalystRanch.com).

In an old building in downtown Chicago, Catalyst Ranch offers a playground that companies can rent for meetings, off-sites, brainstorming sessions, and presentations. The space is filled with color, texture, and fun. Funky retro furniture, art supplies, toys, fabrics, and even materials for prototype design are displayed in a stimulating array of possibilities. In the same way a sparkling lab filled with all the latest equipment appeals to a chemical engineer, Catalyst Ranch is a haven for people engaged in creative processes—the ideal place to stimulate creativity. Business has boomed for Eva, and she has since added a second floor and is constantly asked to open similar facilities in other cities. She is clearly onto an important trend—the need to have inspiring physical spaces to ignite creativity.

In this chapter, we're going to look at some simple ways you can transform your physical environment to help build and sustain creativity. As you'll learn, you don't have to rent new space or build an environment from the ground up to stoke your creative fires. You just have to keep your eyes and your mind open to the possibilities around you.

Breaking out of the Beige Cube Farm

Your physical environment has a direct impact on creativity. I bet you've never heard someone say, "I was sitting in my beige cube with bad florescent lighting, answering a voice mail, watching people rush by, worrying about finishing my Excel spreadsheet and meeting my deadline, when—BAM! I was hit with a lightning bolt of creative inspiration!"

It is no wonder that most companies lack inspiration, when corporate America looks much like a sensory deprivation chamber:

beige walls, faded carpet, high cubes, no windows, and bad lighting, and the only artistic stimulus to be found is the office equipment— your bathroom's shower stall is probably light-years ahead of your office environment when it comes to encouraging original thought.

Aesthetics and physical environment make a clear difference in the occupants' creativity, yet most companies completely overlook this area of easy improvement. Companies invest heavily in having the right tools and equipment—advanced manufacturing systems, state-of-the-art labs, high-bandwidth server farms, top-of-the-line heating and cooling systems. Yet the one aspect of the business that makes all these things possible, creativity and innovation, is largely ignored when it comes to investment. Need a new $100,000 machine? No problem. Need $25 for some Play-Doh? How frivolous . . . forget it.

If you want to see how important the physical work environment is to a creative company, visit Google's headquarters in Mountain View, California. The "Googleplex" looks and feels like an energetic college campus.[2] Going from building to building is easy—jump on a Razor scooter or Segue and head to your destination (just leave it there for the next person to use when you're done—no need to sign it out). Each building is decorated with funky artwork and cool colors, and is well stocked with free food and drinks. Employees are encouraged to bring their friends and family for free meals in the warm and welcoming cafeteria. This dynamic and family-like environment sparks creativity and passion throughout the team.

You can build a creative work environment in just about any setting. At the risk of sounding boastful, I truly believe that ePrize has the coolest office space in Metro Detroit. When I first visited the space in 2004, it was an absolute dump. Built in 1929 as a brewery, the building had been vacant for about fifteen years, and it showed. Rats ran across the cold concrete floors. Remnants of old metal furniture littered the space along with broken windows and an old shaft-style elevator. But the "bones" of the building were fantastic, so I decided to bring it to life.

One year later, our company moved into One ePrize Drive. Broken concrete and filth had given way to exposed brick walls, twenty-foot ceilings, open mechanicals and beams, spiral staircases, and tons of natural light. Walls saturated in color, funky flooring, and specialty lighting have transformed the space from industrial park has-been to SoHo-loft-style standout.

When designing the space, I looked at each room and asked the question, "How can this room stimulate creativity?" Several conference rooms are set up with couches, huge whiteboards, and movable furniture that can be configured differently for different types of meetings. A three-thousand-square-foot rooftop deck loaded with patio furniture (and supported with wireless Web access, of course) provide a nontraditional space for people to do nontraditional work. The central gathering area has bright couches, big comfy chairs, and small work tables. It's a lively space, where people can grab an espresso and interact with their peers, hold quick client chats or short brainstorms—or play pinball, foosball, Xbox and Wii. (If you'd like to take a virtual tour of our space, visit www.ePrize.com.)

The facility draws a steady stream of "wows" from team members and visitors alike. It also sends a strong message to our clients: that we are focused on fresh thinking and that we are not like other companies. Clients leave with a great feeling about working with ePrize.

A creative environment also is an incredible recruiting and retention tool. If you were a bright, creative person at the top of your game and had your choice of nearly any company to work for, what would be attractive to you? A bland, beige cube farm filled with old-school, bureaucratic clutter? Or a surprising and stimulating environment designed to delight and inspire?

Creative environments take many shapes and forms; there's no one set of blueprints for you to follow. Let's look at some of the many ways people and organizations are constructing their own playgrounds for creativity.

Shaking Things Up

The way you use your environment plays an important role in how much creative "juice" it produces. Eric Lefkowski, cofounder of Groupon, is an incredible serial entrepreneur who has taken four companies public, has invested hundreds of millions of dollars in new ventures, and employs thousands of talented people. To keep things fresh, he randomly reassigns seating for hundreds of people in his main Chicago facility on a regular basis (every month or two). Eric believes that this kind of periodic shake-up provides his team with a fresh perspective, a new vantage point. By being moved around, people make different connections with other team members and never get too comfortable. This approach is a powerful stimulus for creativity.[3]

Keeping your team on a steady diet of fresh stimuli can boost original thinking and imagination. Jon Citrin, CEO of the Citrin Group, often moves the art around in his office to give his team something fresh to look at.

There are a number of other ways you can shake things up and stimulate yourself and your team. Try scheduling activities that involve physical movement to get your blood pumping and the oxygen flowing to your brain. Encourage laughter to keep people connected and engaged. Provide fresh, light snacks to give people an alternative to carb-heavy (and mind-numbing) ones. Call for periodic five-minute breaks during which people simply practice deep breathing and relaxation. Whatever tools you use, make sure that you're infusing your work environment with opportunities for stimulating experience to prepare your team, in body and mind, for the creative process.

Spending Time Surrounded by Your Challenge

The extraordinary jazz saxophonist Charlie Parker once disappeared for ten months.[4] With little notice, he left the stage and spent nearly a year in isolation—essentially immersing himself in his art. He didn't read the newspaper, had no contact with outsiders, and spent his days completely focused on his creative passion. When he emerged from this period of deep immersion, his music had changed, and he had become the legend that we remember today.

You don't have to go into hiding for a year to boost your creative chops. Instead, you can try immersing yourself in your Creativity Challenge. Some of the worst business ideas have come out of an ivory tower or lab, where the creators had no connection with their customers. If your target market is ten-year-old boys, you won't reach them by surrounding yourself with forty-something ad agency executives. One of the simplest ways to bridge the gap is by spending a good chunk of time in your customers' world.

IDEO, one of the foremost product design firms in the world, includes an immersion and observation period on every assignment. For example, when IDEO was asked by *Nightline* to demonstrate its creative process on national TV—its challenge was to reinvent the standard grocery store shopping cart—before brainstorming ideas, the team raced to actual grocery stores to carefully observe shoppers in action.

They took note of traffic jams in aisles, watched unconscious patterns made by shoppers, and examined the checkout process. They interviewed shoppers, cart repair people, store managers, and clerks. They immersed themselves in the physical environment of their Creativity Challenge and gathered tremendous insight that, in turn, led to more powerful brainstorming later in the process.

When immersing yourself physically in your Creative Challenge, don't focus on outcomes or predetermined ideas. You need simply to be on a fact-gathering mission and to reserve judgment or conclusions until after the physical immersion period has ended.

Taking It Outside: The Off-Site

The concept of removing yourself from your normal physical surroundings for a period of intense creativity at an off-site location is a long-standing and proven approach. Finding a place that is inspirational, free of distractions, and fresh can make a huge difference in your creativity.

At a 2006 ePrize off-site at a cabin in northern Michigan, we reinvented the architecture for our entire technology platform. Another off-site in Miami Beach in 2007 led to a restructuring of our innovation team that yielded dozens of new products and millions of dollars of revenue. A 2008 trip to Stowe, Vermont, helped us develop a self-service technology concept for international expansion.

If done properly and with lots of planning, off-sites can serve as pivotal moments of creative inspiration. But they can be expensive in both hard dollars and time, so you'll want to ensure that you make every minute count. Here are some best practices for conducting high-impact, creative off-sites:

- **Start with clear objectives.** Make sure you share them with the group in advance. If your off-site is directed at a specific Creativity Challenge, make sure your Creativity Brief is complete and circulated to the team.
- **Establish ground rules.** The rules of engagement can either enable or restrict your group's creativity, so make sure you have

thought through the best way to operate. Here are just some of the ground rules from a recent ePrize off-site:

- Total, absolute, straight-between-the-eyes dialogue.
- Total confidentiality.
- Friendly fire is encouraged.
- Don't start on Chapter 3. (Make sure participants tell the whole story.)
- Dive deep! (Don't only cover issues at the surface.)
- Demand clarity.
- Don't allow the team to go off on tangents and get distracted from the discussion at hand.
- Don't solve for the exceptions.
- No grandiose, absolute, exaggerated statements.
- Strategy: violent debate leads to *action*. How do we take it home?

- **Make the most of intros and endings.** In music, intros and endings to songs are the most memorable aspects to an audience. Begin and end off-sites with something motivational that unites the team and gets them passionate and excited about the future. Really plan these two phases with great care to maximize the impact of your whole off-site.

- **Warm it up.** My favorite way to start an off-site is to prepare a list of powerful historical quotes that are relevant to the key challenges we plan to solve, then have participants read the quotes and discuss how they relate to our challenges. Of course, there are dozens of other warm-up techniques (many mentioned in this book, in fact), so use whatever feels right for you.

- **Create a theme.** I always like to have one overriding theme to the off-site, which could be your Creativity Challenge itself or something more broad, such as Finding a Better Way or Breakthrough Innovation to Drive Breakthrough Results. I also like to have two to four subthemes to serve as guideposts for the agenda and discussion.

- **Sprint and break.** Never go more than two hours without a quick break to stretch, grab a snack, or get some air. During the meetings, however, no cell phones or BlackBerrys allowed. Just total, intense focus followed by periods of rest and recovery.

- **Move outside your comfort zone.** Include some activities— touch football, hiking, and so on—that make people feel a little bit uncomfortable (but that are still safe and business-appropriate, of course). These activities encourage bonding, teamwork, and a sense of play.

- **Get stimulated.** Conduct the off-site in a cool, inspiring location instead of a dimly lit hotel conference center. Have music, food, games, props, toys, and anything else you can think of to stimulate the team. Guest speakers, video clips, interactive sessions, and even live entertainment can make a big impact.

- **Encourage broad participation.** Your role should be that of facilitator, not lecturer. Make sure that the whole team is actively participating. Let others lead some sessions, to give everyone in the group a sense of ownership and to allow others to prepare and contribute meaningful work.

- **Prepare.** Ask people to prepare in advance for a creative experience. Have them read a book or a series of articles in advance of the off-site, or conduct surveys, 360-degree assessments, and advance fact finding in order to make the most of your time together.

Finding the Right Triggers and Symbols

Hemingway went to Key West to write. The Beatles traveled to India for fresh inspiration. Coincidentally, as I write this chapter, I'm sitting in the main reading room of the New York Public Library—a beautiful and inspiring space.

BrightHouse, an Atlanta innovation consulting firm, provides team members five weeks' vacation plus five "Your Days." Your

Days encourage employees to "visit a spot conducive to reflection and letting their neurons rip," according to the CEO. The company also hosts an event called March Forth (falling on March 4th, naturally). On March Fo(u)rth, employees are encouraged to do something they've never done before—skydive, start a novel, take swing dancing lessons, and so on.

Even small creative triggers within your environment can spark big results. In the same way that the smell of food makes your mouth water, specific physical spaces or items can trigger your imagination. When he needed a fresh idea, Thomas Edison liked to sit in his "thinking chair." This was his special place that gave flight to his creativity.

Find your own symbol of creativity and let it launch great ideas. Your trigger can be a specific piece of art or music, or a special word, phrase, quote, or mantra. Craig Erlich, CEO of event marketing powerhouse Pulse 220, had bottles of water labeled as "creativity juice."[5] Even though the team knew it was only water, drinking their creativity juice during meetings somehow inspired better thinking. The key is to use this as a consistent symbol to ignite creativity, in the same way that the national anthem signifies the beginning of a baseball game or a checkered flag symbolizes the end of a Nascar race. Develop your own symbol or anthem and use it consistently. As this ritual sinks in, it will instantly put your team in the right frame of mind and serve as the starting bell for creativity.

In the middle of the daily grind, it is very difficult to focus on the possibilities instead of the task at hand. It is the business equivalent of asking the pilot who is flying an airplane to invent the next type of airplane at the same time. Building a creative environment helps stimulate the senses, makes people think about more than their daily to-do lists, and lets them focus on the creative process.

Project Platypus

Ivy Ross is a renowned sculptor. She also spent six years as Mattel's senior vice president of worldwide girls design and development. Understanding the importance of physical environment, she created an amazing program to harness the company's creativity—Project Platypus.[6]

"We take 12 employees with various skill sets and backgrounds and from all levels of experience," said Ross in an interview. "We give them the task of conceiving and developing a completely new brand. We put them in a separate 2000 square foot building that looks like a playground. The desks are on wheels. There are lots of toys and materials. I like to imagine that a helicopter has picked them up and dropped them someplace completely remote—a totally new environment—even though it is just across the street. For three months they leave their jobs and their titles behind to take part in this experiment."

Ross said she was trying to create a way to work together that is more of a living system than a typical organization structure. For the first two weeks, she doesn't ask anything of the new team members (affectionately called Platipi). Instead, she brings in outside speakers on comedy improv, psychology, and art. The Platypus building has a vibrating sound chair that plays music in order to unite both halves of the brain. The newly formed team goes on field trips, plays games, and actively prepares to be truly creative. The process is thoughtfully designed to encourage a fresh perspective.

The results, according to Ross, have been phenomenal. Five weeks into the first Platypus group, the big wall was covered with thirty-three toy ideas. The goal was to launch one new major toy idea per year, and the group has already blown that number away. Besides creating new products, Project Platypus has reinvigorated the creative spirit at Mattel.

You've seen how taking a group away from their peers and relieving them of normal responsibilities for a short time can spark creativity, but you've also seen that the creative environment can be as big as a national park or as small as an inventor's favorite chair. Whether you repaint the walls, design a common space for creativity, or institute a simple "innovation rotation" whereby team members spend a few weeks in different roles in order to find fresh solutions, explore ways that you can transform your environment to attract and support the process of creativity.

As Mattel's Ivy Ross explained: "We have to find new ways to explore possibilities. In the past, companies could just look at the opportunities afforded by the market at that time. It was stable and predictable. Now, everything is changing. It is very dynamic. We need to focus on the possibilities of a world that does not yet even exist. We need to explore the 'what ifs.'" As you prepare yourself for your own journey into creativity, remember that a creative physical environment is where that exploration begins.

Building Your Creativity Chops

You've seen how preparing your environment for the creative process can yield big rewards. Here are some simple ideas for mixing it up in your environment and seeing what kinds of creative sparks result:

1. **Take a field trip.** Find a location within a one-hour drive from your office and take your team away from the grind for an afternoon. Museums, parks, concerts, or even the local mall are great choices. Expose the group to a fresh set of stimuli that will open up their imaginations.

2. **Build a creativity zone.** Maybe you can't renovate your whole office, but see if you can commandeer one conference room to make it your idea playground. Decorate those beige walls with bright colors. Load the room with art supplies, toys, and games. Trade out folding chairs for beanbags. Most companies have special areas for computer equipment, office supplies, or inventory. Why not have a designated area for creative thinking? For a minimal investment, you can transform a small area of your office into a space for creating big new ideas.

3. **Change it up.** To the extent you are able, have your team members change where they sit. Change the wall color, furniture, lighting, and any other variables within your control. Change them, and then change them again shortly thereafter. The idea of constant physical change (even as simple as repositioning the furniture in your office for a new view) can help you and your team embrace change and fresh thinking.

DISCOVER

7

•——

Discovering the Ways of Creativity

So many of our dreams at first seem impossible, then they seem improbable, and then when we summon the will, they soon become inevitable.

—CHRISTOPHER REEVE

A few years ago at my son's school, there was a power outage caused by a squirrel that (most unfortunately) got caught in the electrical wires. Typically, a teacher would quickly move past this sort of annoyance and get on with class. Instead, Noah's teacher had the kids put on their coats and go looking for the culprit.

A thirty-minute hunt in the adjacent woods yielded the desired outcome: they found the hapless animal. After a heartfelt round of "euwwww's," the teacher had her students form a circle around the dead squirrel. She asked one child to describe what he saw. "A dead squirrel," replied the nine-year-old, naturally enough. Then the teacher asked the next kid in the circle the same question, but with two differences: "Describe in *detail* what you see, from the perspective of a *scientist*."

The girl proceeded to explain in detail things like bones, fur, and blood. The teacher asked the next student to keep the detail, but describe what he saw from the perspective of an artist. The result was a description of the squirrel in terms of color, texture, and depth. Next up was a description from the perspective of a poet. Then an engineer. And so it went, around the circle;

each participant was asked to describe the scene from a different perspective.

What this brilliant teacher was demonstrating to her students was the stage of creativity that is *discovery*—and Discover is the third phase of the Disciplined Dreaming process. In this stage, you break free of the straitjacket of "We've always done it that way" or "This is our usual approach" or "We don't have the luxury of trying something new."

Legendary jazz trumpeter Miles Davis believed that musical creativity was an act of discovery. Simply put, he thought that the music already existed, and it was his role as an artist to discover it. Throughout the four decades of his extraordinary career, Davis constantly searched for inspiration from a wide variety of sources, exploring new boundaries at every turn, going well beyond the normal confines of the jazz of his day. We've seen how your mental, cultural, and physical state can boost your creative abilities by preparing you for the creative journey. That journey is all about discovery. In this chapter, we'll look at several ideas and activities for guiding you in the Discover phase of the creative process.

Looking Through a Different Lens

Looking at a problem from a new perspective, perhaps by playing a particular role, as my son and those other young students found, is an excellent way to discover creative new approaches and solutions. I call this approach "a Different Lens," and it involves, quite simply, looking with fresh eyes at a problem you're thinking about.

In your next brainstorming session, for example, think about the issue from the perspective of a musician—or a villain or an architect. By role playing, you can find that fresh perspective yourself, even when looking at problems you've been struggling with for a long time.

At ePrize, we've used this technique—with a twist. A little while ago, we had to make an important sales presentation to a client. After hours of work, we were stuck; our approach lacked pizzazz. So we decided to pretend that we were characters from the TV series *Mad Men,* a television series set in a 1960s advertising agency. Our lead creative director took on the persona of Don Draper, the suave, polished storyteller who heads the agency's creative department. The rest of us adopted the roles of the other characters in the show.

Our pitch became significantly better. By approaching our Creativity Challenge (to win the client) with a fresh and different perspective, we discovered new possibilities and approaches. In the end, our presentation to the client used a number of the insights we gained from that creative exercise. And we won a significant piece of business in a highly competitive shoot-out.

Jon Citrin, the CEO and founder of the Citrin Group (mentioned earlier), uses a great technique called the Blocker to see his own ideas and approaches from a different perspective.[1] At the beginning of most of his meetings, he selects someone on his team to play the role of the Blocker. That person's job is to passionately disagree with Jon on every issue. The Blocker must confront the boss at every turn; he's protected by his role from offending Jon or getting in trouble. It's just his job. The technique creates lively debate and forces real conversation around issues instead of a room full of agreement. It also makes everyone on the team take a closer, more critical look at Jon's ideas.

"I can't grow our company by myself," says Dan Gilbert, owner of the Cleveland Cavaliers and chairman and founder of Quicken Loans, a company whose three thousand employees are strongly encouraged to challenge everything and everyone, including Dan.[2]

"That's why we need all six thousand eyeballs looking critically at our business and finding new and creative ways to improve it. The opportunities for growth are everywhere, and we need to have a culture that encourages people to speak up. Why hire smart, talented people for their judgment and then never allow them to use it?"

Using this role-playing technique of deliberately adopting a different perspective can help us get past our natural fear of speaking up and challenging opinions from within a hierarchy. As Wayne Dyer says, "If you change the way you look at things, the things you look at change."

Capitalizing on Inflection Points

Andy Grove, the former chairman and CEO of Intel, often said that opportunities are hidden in inflection points—a point where one social or business trend changes trajectory and starts off in a new direction.[3] Points of change have marked business breakthroughs more often than not, and offer perceptive entrepreneurs irresistible chances to launch new enterprises. By carefully examining inflection points, we can discover spectacular business opportunities.

These sorts of pivotal changes are easy to spot in retrospect. Think of the printing press or the automobile or the Internet. Each of these disruptive technologies created billions of dollars of wealth for those who helped with their birth, and led to countless follow-on businesses and professions. Social changes, such as the civil rights movement and globalization, are inflection points that unleashed extraordinary opportunities for those perceptive enough to realize their significance early on.

Today inflection points occur constantly. They happen when we see changes in political administrations, climate, consumer preferences, foreign relations, technology, health and fitness, travel habits, fashion, and music. The trick is to spot the point of change—the point where you can define a "pre" and a "post" condition that signals an inflection point. The entire trend-spotting industry labors to help us see these inflection points while they're first developing, so that we can capitalize on the opportunities they create.

Opportunities can lie at the intersection of multiple inflection points or trends. Take the green movement, add the desire to reduce our reliance on foreign oil for both cost and geopolitical reasons, and throw in the enduring consumer fondness for stylish cars, and what do you get? The Tesla.

Tesla Motors will succeed or fail because of the power of these combined inflection points. The Tesla Roadster has a range of 244 miles on a single 3.5-hour battery charge. It's a fully electric car, boasting no emissions, no need for gasoline, and no use of foreign oil. The car accelerates from 0 to 60 mph in under four seconds and combines that power with a beautiful design and a choice of thirteen funky colors. In an era when car dealers are burdened with months of excess inventory, Tesla enjoys a two-year waiting list—for a $90,000 car!

The car is replete with other innovations that leverage inflection points: a unique PIN that starts the car, making it nearly impossible to hotwire (inflection point: cool cars are often stolen); single-occupancy access to all carpool lanes (inflection point: people hate getting stuck in traffic, but often have to drive alone); and "valet mode," which limits the number of miles a valet can drive the car (inflection point: people hate it when valets go for joyrides).

Inflection points don't always need to lead to a new invention, however; sometimes a twist on an old idea is enough.

In Japan, a savvy entrepreneur noticed an emerging trend.[4] Large numbers of Japanese men who lived outside Tokyo and worked in the city would leave work at the end of the day, head to a nearby bar for some drinks, and then catch the last train out of the city. With their destination an hour or more away, they would usually fall asleep, waking up far past their desired stop. With no return train service and a several-hundred-dollar cab fare in their future, these workers were in a tight spot.

But not anymore. Today, a hotel specifically built to cater to this emerging market is located right across the street from the end-of-the-line train station. By noticing a trend, the hotel owner was able to capitalize on a new opportunity. The land at the end of the train line was cheap to acquire and build on, and the entrepreneur was able to charge premium rates for the hotel rooms, because they were still less expensive than the dreaded cab ride.

What inflection points are occurring in the lives of your customers? In your industry? With your competition? In related technology? By training yourself to watch for important new trends, you can find creative ways to capitalize on these inflection points and change the direction of your career, business, or industry.

Discovering New Potential in a Borrowed Idea

George de Mestral was frustrated. He had just returned from a hunting trip with his dog in the Alps. The source of his annoyance was a collection of tiny burrs that he'd picked up in the woods, covering his clothes and his pet. George happened to be an inventor, so he took one of those burrs and studied it under a microscope and noticed tiny hooks that connected to the fabric of his clothes and his dog's fur. George started to think about taking this same concept and using it as a fastener—as a competitor for the zipper. The product Velcro was born that day, a spectacular example of the Borrowed Idea.[5]

The concept of discovery through the Borrowed Idea is simple: find something that is working in one area of life and apply the same principle to the problem at hand. Enormous fortunes have been made employing this simple yet powerful technique.

Many of the best borrowed ideas come from nature. A metalworking company in the Midwest recently studied sharks and piranhas in order to model its next generation of cutting tools on the teeth and jaws of these formidable fish. Ant farms have been studied to find better ways to manage traffic in urban cities. Chirping birds have inspired countless songs and dances.

In fact, I founded ePrize from a borrowed idea. I was eager to build a company that designed and managed interactive sweepstakes and promotions, but needed something to get started. I started thinking about the big prizes and how a huge amount of money goes to fund one grand prize. The real benefit to an advertiser in running a sweepstakes is to capture the imaginations of thousands (or millions) of participants who have the chance to win. I also realized that consumers wouldn't respond unless there was a big enough prize. Nobody wanted to win a ballpoint pen or a Frisbee. It had to be a car or a luxury vacation or exotic jewelry.

So I put the Borrowed Idea to work. One proven business model was the timeshare concept: one expensive fixed asset with multiple people sharing the cost. In the early 1990s, the concept worked for timeshare jets. Each user owned a fraction of the jet, thus sharing the large fixed overhead costs. *Why not apply the same concept to sweepstakes?* I thought.

As a result, I launched ePrize with a single product: Pooled Drawings. I set up a system that allowed advertisers to share the cost of the big prize. The idea was that each client could offer an eye-catching prize without having to write a correspondingly eye-catching check. Participants had a legitimate chance to win the top prize, but the clients could spread the odds across multiple companies. A winner could come from any one of my clients' sweepstakes. Of course, we fully disclaimed the pooling concept in the official rules and regulations. If you think about it, it is very much like a multistate lottery. There are multiple entry points, everyone gets a fair shot, and there's only one grand prize winner.

By using the Borrowed Idea concept, I was able to launch my company with a unique offering. Although our products and services have evolved greatly over the years, it all began with one idea: a borrowed idea.

It's been well reported that Howard Shultz got the idea for Starbucks while sitting in a quaint café in Italy.[6] From the memory of that café, Shultz created a concept that wasn't solely about getting a hot coffee but also about an experience. The driving success factors were high quality, beautiful presentation, and a warm feeling inside the patrons. Shultz's borrowed idea made retailing history.

You'll find that opportunities to borrow ideas are everywhere— if you make it your business to discover them.

A Borrowed Idea from Halloween

Harvey Kanter, the CEO of the outdoor apparel retailer (and e-tailer) Moosejaw, told me that early in his career, he was brought in to help a troubled retailer whose management lacked discipline and control.[7] He found that there was enough inventory on hand to fill five large stores, but the company had only three in its local market. The cost of the inventory was killing its bottom line.

Harvey recalled the previous Halloween and a store called Halloween USA that rented vacant retail space cheap to sell costumes and accessories for the Halloween season only. He decided to borrow the idea and use it as a way to reduce his extra inventory. With no advertising budget, he used word-of-mouth marketing and hoped he could sell the excess inventory over a six-week period. The idea was so successful that he completely sold out his inventory in three days! There were huge lines out the door, and the police had to come in to direct traffic. His borrowed idea of creating customer urgency, low prices, and a limited supply generated buzz, demand, and, most important, sales.

Turning a Problem Upside Down

Nintendo was an early entrant into the video game market. In 1985, it achieved tremendous success with the launch of the Nintendo Entertainment System (NES) that showcased games like Super Mario Brothers. The year 1989 brought the breakthrough handheld game device known as the Nintendo Game Boy. Soon enough, however, Nintendo's dominance faded, and the best the company could manage was a distant third place to Microsoft Xbox and Sony PlayStation.

As Microsoft and Sony pumped hundreds of millions of dollars into R&D to create cooler graphics, sound, and game play, the smaller and less well funded Nintendo was at a pivotal point in its evolution and, possibly, its struggle for survival. Its leaders decided to use a nontraditional approach to the problem at hand: the Upside Down. Rather than fighting the battle for the best graphics or sound, the company decided to turn the problem around and go for something new: the Nintendo Wii.

Nintendo changed the problem it was solving. Instead of building a device to support better games, the company built a device with a better game experience. In fact, Wii games have feebler graphics and sound than the Xbox and PlayStation. But the Wii game experience is far superior to that of its rivals. The Wii uses an infrared sensor to make an active game experience. Instead of sitting still and furiously clicking buttons, players use lifelike motions with their controllers. When the game system launched, it was sold out for months, and the Wii quickly became the best-selling game system in the country.

The Upside Down concept is all about turning a problem around and solving for something different in order to succeed. To discover opportunities for using the Upside Down to solve your

Creativity Challenge, begin the process by using an "Instead of" variation of the "What if" question you learned about in Chapter Four. Here are some examples:

- "*Instead of* trying to offer our customers lower rates at our bank, *what if* we offered the best service?"
- "*Instead of* monitoring our employees' time sheets, *what if* we created a reward system that encouraged them to be more productive and at the same time provided them with more control of their schedules?"
- "*Instead of* producing all our products centrally, *what if* we subdivided our production into regional centers to offer more customization and closer access to customers?"
- "*Instead of* running TV and radio ads this holiday season, *what if* we launched an interactive experience or contest that drove deep consumer engagement while creating lots of PR and buzz?"
- "*Instead of* competing head-to-head in the commodity diamond business, *what if* we created a premium, branded diamond?"

Hearts on Fire diamonds offer a real-life example of a savvy entrepreneur using the Upside Down approach to redefine the playing field in an established industry. Most people would agree that diamonds are diamonds are diamonds—commodities whose values are driven by cut, clarity, caret weight, and color.

Glenn Rothman, the CEO of Hearts on Fire, seized an opportunity to stand out in the increasingly commoditized world of diamonds through a remarkable branding and positioning campaign.[8] Hearts on Fire diamonds are marketed as being the best in the world. The company uses a special cutting tool and boasts the tagline: "The world's most perfectly cut diamonds." Hearts on Fire demands that the backdrop velvet in display cases in stores be its special brilliant purple and that retailers use custom lighting to make its display stand out. The company provides jewelers with special Hearts on Fire magnification viewers to show customers its diamonds. The company has enjoyed 30 percent annualized growth over the last eleven years, and its diamonds command a 50 percent premium over its rivals.

Let's look at one more example. Tony Sosnick is the founder and CEO of Anthony Logistics for Men, a cosmetics line. The company sells fancy shaving cream, lotion, shampoo, and other products for men. Let's look at how Tony used the Upside Down to turn a major setback into pay dirt.

In early 2008, Tony received what he believed to be a game-changing opportunity when Walmart asked him to develop a custom line of products to be sold exclusively at its stores. Tony and his team got to work developing the concept and, six months later, flew to Bentonville to present their work. But the new head buyer at Walmart had no interest in the new product line. Tony had invested more than $150,000 in the development of this special line, making for a long flight back to New York City.

But Tony wasn't willing to write off the loss, so he deployed the Upside Down technique. Rather than trying to figure out how to convince Walmart to buy his product, he decided to turn the situation around by taking the same product and marketing it to another retailer. With some simple changes to make the packaging more upscale and the products a little fancier smelling, Tony was soon meeting with the head buyer of posh retailer Barneys New York. Instead of creating a custom line of *low*-end products, he turned his strategy around to produce to a custom line of *high*-end products. The brand went on to become a best seller at these high-end stores at a very premium price point. By turning the problem upside down, Tony was able to transform a very expensive loss into an even bigger profit.

Jazz musicians use the Upside Down constantly as a way to find new ground. In fact, there is a whole concept known as *harmonic substitution,* through which a musician has the liberty to swap one chord or scale for another. Instead of playing a G7 chord, for example, the musician can swap it for a Db7. Instead of playing C major scale, a musician might try an E harmonic minor scale. It's a way of inverting the challenge and discovering creativity in new places.

One of the concepts I love to try myself when performing jazz is to turn the entire song around. If a song is written as a ballad, I like to try playing it in a fast swing tempo. If it has a blues feel, I'll try it with a Latin feel. I often find that the most creative moments—and the best audience response—come in those moments when I'm able to turn a song upside down to find something completely new. And if it doesn't work out, the old jazz cats will tell you, "Hey man. If you play a wrong note, don't worry. Just play it twice more with conviction and the audience will think you did it on purpose."

These are just a few examples of the ways you can upend limited expectations by changing the nature of the problem before you. As you build your creative muscles, you'll find many opportunities for using the Upside Down to transform disaster into discovery.

Putting Patterns to Use

In the game of chess, the difference between a Grandmaster and a mere expert lies not in skill or intelligence but in the ability to recognize patterns. The Grandmaster recognizes three times the number of patterns, and in turn can beat the expert consistently in game after game.

The ability to recognize and use patterns has long meant the difference between success and failure, and has long been a source of creativity and innovation. Dave Brubeck's jazz standard "Take Five" was based on the noise pattern the composer heard in a train leaving its station. Military air strikes in World War II were based on the flight patterns of birds in formation. In fact, consider the classic military strategy book *The Art of War,* by Sun Tzu, that sits on the bookshelves of thousands of business leaders, artists, and educators throughout the world today. The book is a classic—not for its literal meaning, but because it identifies a series of *patterns* that can be applied to develop strategies in an effective and predictable way. Patterns are a powerful source of creativity and can lead to breakthrough thinking and results.

In the early 1980s, after focus group testing, the Minnetonka Corporation knew it had a likely hit with its new product, SoftSoap. Its big fear was that larger competitors like Procter & Gamble could easily copy and outspend SoftSoap when it came to advertising and promotion.

At the time, there were only two companies that manufactured the plastic pumps required to make SoftSoap usable in the home. Rather than trying to take the bigger corporation head-on, Minnetonka bought up the world supply of these pumps—over one hundred million of them. When the product launched, competitors were left helpless for eighteen months until they could secure another source for the pumps. Minnetonka had adopted an ancient war strategy in which the attacker defeats the opponent by cutting off his supplies rather than through head-to-head combat. This strategy, driven by pattern recognition, allowed SoftSoap to get a big head start and secure consumer acceptance and, ultimately, loyalty.

Business patterns are virtually endless, and they are easy to discover and apply as cycles repeat. Burger King launched a campaign called "Have It Your Way" back in the early 1980s to compete with the formulaic McDonald's, and began what would become a pattern of offering on-demand customer customization. Cold Stone Creamery followed suit to create a "have it your way" ice cream parlor, allowing consumers to add whatever ingredients they wanted and have the final ice cream treat smashed together before their eyes. Dale and Thomas Popcorn Company did the same thing, allowing users to mix and match funky flavors.

Zazzle, an entrepreneurial company in Redwood City, California, took that trend one step further. Zazzle is an on-demand manufacturer, offering billions of customized items (22.9 billion as of 2010) manufactured and shipped within twenty-four hours, including T-shirts, mugs, skateboards, and tennis shoes. Zazzle receives over a hundred thousand orders each day, with an average turnaround time from order to finished product of seventeen minutes. Started in 2005 and expecting to reach over $100 million in sales in 2010, Zazzle identified a powerful pattern and applied it in a new (and big) way.

In studying business cycles and patterns for success across industries, I noticed that most had a big annual conference: the North American Auto Show in the automotive sector, for example, or Comdex in the technology world. There's even an annual event for event planners. Because the world of interactive promotions was new in the early 2000s, there was no such event for our industry. I began to think of ways that I could create my own version of the annual event at ePrize to win a significant advantage. My solution: the Interactive Promotion Summit. What a tremendous opportunity, I thought, to create and own the dominant annual conference in our industry. It would be like GM owning the auto show.

The challenge was to establish a legitimate and credible annual conference and not make it appear to be an ePrize commercial. I referred back to the classic Sun Tzu pattern that described how larger forces win against smaller forces on their own territory, and solved the puzzle. To legitimize the conference, I needed to invite my competitors.

My colleagues told me I was nuts. "You can't invite our competition into a room with our clients," my team yelled. "They'll steal our customers!" I viewed the situation differently, however, and we launched the Interactive Promotion Summit in 2004.

My company stacked the deck in terms of content. No one from ePrize officially presented (I was the emcee, but there were no formal presentations); major brands presented case studies of cutting-edge campaigns. Of course, these were our clients who were raving about their ePrize promotions. The conference grew over the next few years to reach five hundred annual attendees, most of which were major brand advertisers. Our competitors also showed up. After all, how could they miss the key annual industry event?

They were completely ineffective at attracting any business, but their presence legitimized the conference. It enabled us to convince *PROMO* magazine (our industry's trade journal) to hold an award ceremony at the conference. It also allowed me to sell sponsorship to the event, which ended up covering 85 percent of the cost. Today, owning the main event in our industry is a key asset of our company. This gigantic win for my organization all started by recognizing a pattern and finding a way to make it our own.

■ ■ ■

Creativity exists all around us. I encourage you to put these discovery techniques to work in order to find creativity wherever it hides within your organization, industry, or other creative pursuit. The Discover process takes bravery, curiosity, and awareness. But, as is true in the exploration to discover new lands, there are enormous rewards for those willing to seek the sources of creativity.

Building Your Creativity Chops

If you haven't used your creative muscles for a while, you might feel like a musician who hasn't touched his instrument in weeks. Your creativity is still within you; you just have to wake it up and get it ready to wail. Use these ideas to take the first steps:

1. **Immerse yourself in magazines.** Go to a local bookstore and select ten magazines that you don't usually read. Find the strangest publications you can, covering topics or hobbies that are completely foreign to you. Consider each magazine as you would a whole new world. What is striking about the ads? How is the language different? What is unusual about the design and imagery? Once you've had a chance to become immersed, try approaching your Creativity Challenge from the perspective of an avid reader of that magazine. If you chose *Photography Today*, for example, ask how a professional photographer would approach your problem. Then try *Cigar Aficionado, Florida Lifestyles,* and *Modern Trumpet Weekly*.

2. **Find the inflection points.** What general inflection points can you identify within your life, your customers' lives, your industry, your competitors' offerings, or in related technologies? Periodically spend three minutes identifying and listing as many of these inflection points as you can. The lists will powerfully inspire your creativity.

STEP FOUR

•

IGNITE

8

Generating Creative Sparks

Ideas are like rabbits. You get a couple and learn how to handle them, and pretty soon you have a dozen.

—JOHN STEINBECK

There are some things in life that just scare the heck out of you. For some people, their worst fear is public speaking. For others, it could be heights, small spaces, bears, germs, or even love. Some people—maybe even you—fear the blank page or any situation in which they must spark their creative process (technical term: *getting-creative-now-o-phobia*).

Irrational phobias can unfortunately cripple people, preventing them from reaching their potential and truly enjoying life. To unleash your creativity and that of your team, you need to break through the barriers that stall your creative process. In this chapter, I'll share some proven techniques that you can immediately put to use to help your blank canvas, page, musical staff paper, stage, spreadsheet, or presentation come to life. We'll explore powerful tools from both the art world and the business world that you can use to set off the sparks of creativity in you and your group, so that you never again have to sit smoldering on square one.

Protecting Those First, Fragile Sparks

An object in motion stays in motion, while an object at rest tends to stay at rest.

—NEWTON'S FIRST LAW OF MOTION

If you are staring down the barrel of a large creative project, the challenge can feel daunting. Taking the first step of a mountain climb, beginning a new diet, or registering for the first course of graduate school can be scary and distracting. Many people size up the challenge and, unfortunately, let fear overpower them and keep them from moving forward.

Think about your creative potential as a raging forest fire. Extraordinary heat and furious energy, growing and spreading with explosive power. Forest fires don't magically appear out of the blue. There's no such thing as an entire forest spontaneously combusting in the blink of an eye. Instead, they begin with a *spark*. The spark could come from a cigarette butt, a leftover campfire, or a thunderstorm, but a single spark is required to begin. The same is true for your creativity, and specifically for beginning a creative project.

One of the most common stumbling blocks is the feeling that you need to imagine and perfectly design the entire creative solution *before* beginning work. This couldn't be further from the truth. In fact, nearly every creative project I've ever worked on or researched came to life as an evolutionary process rather than as a single lightning bolt of perfect inspiration. The writer of a screenplay, for example, may have a general idea, but rarely knows the entire detailed plotline before putting pen to paper. Creative projects of all sizes tend to bounce around, morph, and change directions along the way to their final state.

The creative act is nonlinear, and may not be fully realized until a work is near completion—which makes it critically important to allow yourself to begin without knowing all the answers. Often the first part of generating an idea isn't formulating a complete and thorough concept, but rather to look for sparks.

A creative spark need not be a fully baked idea. In fact, most aren't. Look for little flashes of inspiration or thoughts to get your work under way. If you are an author working on a new novel, for example, a spark may be simply the name or even hair color of the protagonist. If you are working to reinvent a workflow system of a production line, a spark could be a simple diagram of the current system with indications of the inefficient points in the process. If you are working on a new ad campaign, a spark could be a collection of a dozen of your favorite campaigns by other companies. A chef's spark may be a single ingredient, such as cilantro, to begin a new chicken recipe. A product design spark may be a simple idea for a new grip on a toothbrush.

When trying to spark your creative flame, remember these two points: (1) start with a number of small sparks, no matter how incomplete, to begin the creative process; and (2) be very careful not to quickly extinguish those sparks.

The heat from a cigarette butt can easily be extinguished compared to the fury of a full-blown forest fire. Similarly, your initial creative sparks are fragile and need support and nurturing to grow into your own creative fire. The most common way to prematurely kill your sparks is to switch into left-brain, analytical mode. Your little, young, fragile spark is no match for the brutal attack of fear-based thinking. We give human babies eighteen years (or more) of nurturing before they stand on their own, yet we expect the smallest hatchling of an idea to fly out of the nest immediately. Give your sparks care and feeding so that they can grow into fruitful and more mature ideas.

Twelve Ways to Strike Sparks of Creativity

There are many tools you can use to light a fire—matches, lighter fluid, a torch. Here are twelve tools and techniques that will help you generate your own creative sparks.

Imbizo Groups

Imbizo is the Zulu expression for "gathering." Imbizo groups—gatherings of people from diverse backgrounds and disciplines who have come together to simply discuss an idea—are one of the most powerful ways to generate creative sparks. These groups are free-form and have no specific end goal in mind, other than exploring. The key to having a successful Imbizo is to let go of the outcome and simply allow the discussion to ensue.

Imagine you are sitting with a diverse group of people, and your Creativity Challenge is to streamline the check-in and drop-off process for your client, a rental car company. Rather than posing the challenge to the team and brainstorming ideas, the Imbizo group would simply discuss the topic of rental car experiences. The discussion might wander from how reservations are made to specific bottlenecks in the system to what people enjoy or dislike about the process. Some people in your group (because it is highly diverse) may have never rented a car before. Because they are not saddled with history and biases, they will offer a completely different perspective than a frequent business traveler. Perhaps an artist will have a certain take on things, a food science chemist another.

Let go of the outcome and encourage free-flowing dialogue on the general topic of your Creativity Challenge. Bring lots of snacks and lots of paper to write down all the sparks that will burst from the conversation.

The Hot Potato

Just as with the childhood game of Hot Potato, put everyone in a circle—except for one person who will be taking furious notes. Toss a Nerf football (instead of a potato) to a random person in the group, who is required to shout out one idea for a new or better service you can offer your clients. Anyone who catches the ball has to shout out an idea that's no more than one sentence long—she isn't allowed to think about it, analyze it, or contemplate her phrasing. Each person has to think fast, shoot from the hip, and let his spontaneous creativity fly. This fast-paced exercise creates a situation that removes obstacles, blockers, and fear.

Let the ideas flow for fifteen minutes. Some will be crazy, some will be stupid, and some will be astonishingly brilliant. When people get into the rhythm and let down their guard, beautiful ideas come more naturally. When we reviewed the output from doing the Hot Potato at ePrize, we discovered that this single exercise had yielded not only more but better ideas than other brainstorming sessions.

The Start Ain't Always the Start

When most people face a big project, they assume they need to start on "page one." If you were a writer, for example, you might think your job is to begin your writing process by writing the first page of the book. But staring at that starting point can dampen, rather than ignite, your creativity. To avoid that dampening effect, remember that there's a difference between starting to work and a creative project's "beginning."

The writer may choose to begin the project in the middle of the book. A musician may begin her composition with a catchy ending. The creative process need not be linear for either art or business. Try approaching creativity from different points in the work, and you may just uncover some hot new sparks, not to mention overcoming the fear of the blank page.

The Wrong Answer

You are working to solve a challenge and find the right answer. So what better way to find that right answer than to begin by finding the wrong one?

When you are facing the daunting task of fixing a problem or inventing something new, the challenge often feels overwhelming. We are all socialized to avoid making mistakes and are reluctant to raise our hands unless we know we're right. There is such a stigma around being wrong that it's difficult to imagine a more humiliating situation than being completely wrong in front of your colleagues. As we've seen, this fear does a whammy on the creative process and often restricts people's willingness to try new things or share new ideas.

To uncover some sparks and kick off the creative process, try searching for the wrong answer instead of the right one. Generate ideas to solve the polar opposite of your Creativity Challenge. Here are some examples:

- "How could we win an award for the *worst* customer service?"
- "What would have to change to make our internal manufacturing systems 30 percent more *inefficient*?"
- "What are some ideas for an ad campaign that would never win any awards, get lost in the shuffle, and end up with the *worst* direct-response rate in our company's history?"
- "How could we increase labor costs while decreasing customer satisfaction?"

Although these questions may seem silly, they are also extremely nonthreatening. Brainstorming around questions like these will be fun and will inevitably generate a lot of laughs—but after careful examination, they will also generate a bunch of creative sparks. If you look at your answers and then flip their meaning around, you may just end up with some powerful ammunition with which to go after your actual Creativity Challenge.

Stick It to the Man

Just by the title, you know this exercise is going to be fun. We've all felt kicked around at some point in our lives. Perhaps it was the school bully or an overbearing boss or the seemingly unbeatable competition. Here's your chance to get back. In this exercise, it is your job to be irreverent. To pick a fight. To shake things up.

To begin, think about your Creativity Challenge and what you could do to really piss people off. Start with your boss. What ideas would send her into cardiac arrest? Next, move on to your competition. Think of all the things you could do to stick a thumb in their eye, pour salt in their wounds, and send them off the deep end.

Now that you are having fun, don't stop there. What would create environmental outrage? What would engender a political explosion? Can you think of anything so obnoxious and racy that a riot might ensue? Don't hold back. Here's the one time when your goal is to be politically incorrect. This type of thinking forces you way outside your normal thought process (your normal thought process being your greatest enemy) and will help you generate some very wild creative sparks. Once you have a nice list of offensive ideas, look them over to see what *inoffensive* ideas they trigger. Finding alternatives will be easy. You accomplished the hard part in the midst of your mischievous fun—breaking through old thought patterns and letting your creative abilities shine.

Get Stimulated

Just as a double espresso or a couple of Red Bulls will stimulate your body (at least in the short term), stimulating your creativity is a great way to overcome the blank page. Start by clearing your mind and putting your Creativity Challenge on the back burner. Sometimes you need to relax your mind to unlock your creativity. From there, expose yourself and your team to a Costco-size helping of stimulation. You can use any of the many ideas for stimulating activities and environments we've discussed throughout this book.

The idea is to step away from your Creativity Challenge for a period of stimulation, ranging from a couple minutes to a couple days. From there, refocus on your Creativity Challenge, and you'll find fresh sparks of creativity filling that scary blank page. The more you stimulate your brain, the more you will develop your never-ending ability to learn, grow, and create.

The Time Capsule

Imagine that you and your team have a time machine. When you're struggling to ignite a creative spark, jump in your time machine and go back fifty years. How would people from that era approach your Creativity Challenge? What about a hundred years back? Or five hundred years?

Now go forward in your time machine. How would you approach your challenge fifty years into the future? What ideas might you use from the vantage point of a hundred years into the future? With any new technology you can imagine and with a whole host of new competitors, how would your group from the future begin the job at hand? Shifting your perspective to the future or the past can open up your mind with fresh ideas and help generate some sparks to kick your creative process into high gear.

The Hemingway Bridge

One of my favorite techniques to keep creative momentum is the Hemingway Bridge.[1] Ernest Hemingway would find that sometimes he'd finish writing a chapter and be completely spent. He had poured his heart and soul into the chapter and was satisfied and relieved once the chapter was complete, but this sense of accomplishment made beginning the next chapter very difficult. Sometimes he would get stuck while starting the next chapter and faced the same frustration with the blank page that any of us feel at the beginning of a project. He developed a technique—known as the Hemingway Bridge—to avoid this start-and-stop challenge.

Rather than ending a chapter and then beginning the next day with a blank page, Hemingway would write the first paragraph of the next chapter before ending his day's work. The next day, he had a head start. Having the initial thoughts already started on the page allowed him to pick up midstream rather than from a dead stop. In the evening, he would think about where the newly formed idea would evolve so that when he began work the next day, it was much easier for him to dive in and create great work without needing to push himself off from square one again.

You can use the Hemingway Bridge to keep the momentum going throughout your creative project. As you complete various phases or subtasks of your Creativity Challenge, simply start the very early beginning of the next one before putting down your work or ending your meeting. Bridge your ideas into the next element of the project, and you will have a much easier time picking it up at a later time.

Personas

At ePrize, we use the concept of personas to spark our creativity when building solutions and proposals for clients. Different clients care about different things. One client may care passionately about visual design but is bored to death when talking about metrics and reporting. Another client may be consumed with security and infrastructure, but couldn't care less about user flow and consumer interface. What we realized is that trying to sell a client on features or benefits that didn't matter to that person was a waste of time and hurt our chances rather than helped. To help us better target our message, we created a handful of client personas.

Artsy Anna is really into visual design. ROI Ronnie cares only about return on investment. Technical Tommy wants to know all about bits and bytes. Security Sally will never buy unless she knows her company is safe. We ended up building out ten key customer personas, complete with drawings, names, and detailed descriptions. We then trained our salespeople and product development folks to focus their energies on specific personas rather than just customers in general. This drove better closing rates with our salespeople and better products from our innovation team. The personas helped us better connect with our customers.

You can use personas in a similar way to spark creativity. Nearly all Creativity Challenges have an impact on people. Your target audience could be a customer, supplier, investor, employee, boss, the media, and so on. Rather than thinking about a generic, one-size-fits-all audience, try crafting personas. For example: Investor Ivan. Age fifty-two, lives in Chicago. Two kids in college. Balanced portfolio, but likes to take some risks. Appreciates straight talk and hates to be surprised. Drives a late-model Lincoln. Has a summer home on a lake in Wisconsin. Jogs three times a week, but is still fifteen pounds overweight thanks to fancy client dinners and the junk food he eats while traveling for business.

As you can see, the more detail the better. You want to really get inside the head of your audience and make them into a specific person you can relate to instead of a faceless, nameless target. From there, you can focus your creativity by asking such questions as "What would Ivan appreciate more, option 1 or option 2?" "How would Ivan respond to our new product launch that could triple our business but carries significant risk?" "What typeface for our annual report would project confidence to Ivan?"

A great way to get started with a creative project is to have one person play one of your target audience personas, and another play the role of a company representative. Hold a few impromptu conversations, with the others in your group taking notes. Observe the natural flow and look for nuggets that may spark your creative process.

Provocation

Creativity legend Edward de Bono suggests using the technique of provocation to spark creative ideas.[2] This is a tool to break established patterns and find unorthodox ideas. To begin, make a provocative (often "stupid") statement, such as "Houses should not have roofs." From there, explore the ins and outs of the statement and provoke your team into a lively discussion.

You could start by exploring the consequences of the statement. Here's an example: Would people need to carry umbrellas to the bathroom? What would the benefits be? What special circumstances would actually make this a sensible solution? What would need to happen to actually make this, or something like it, work? What would happen if a sequence of events were changed?

The objective here is to generate sparks, not fully developed ideas or solutions. Provocation will help you look at your situation from a completely different angle. The absurd may quickly morph into your best ideas, so think of this simply as an incubator of original thought.

Dagnabbits

Ross Sanders is the executive director of Bizdom U, a nonprofit entrepreneurial academy to help promote hope and economic prosperity in urban centers.[3] He asks his students, partners, and contributors to keep an eye out for "dagnabbits"—moments when they feel frustrated about a situation, product, or service. A dagnabbit is akin to stubbing your toe. It's that flash of gosh-darn-it disappointment or frustration that makes you wish the world were different. (Of course, feel free to substitute any expletive you choose.)

Rather than just getting annoyed and moving on, keep a running list of these moments. Those lists can become one of your greatest sources of creative sparks. In fact, many of the greatest inventions came directly out of dagnabbit moments. Pierre Omidyar founded eBay when he was frustrated that there was no easy way to build his Pez collection online. Frederick Smith was outraged that there was no reliable way to send overnight packages, so he launched Federal Express. Don Wetzel was upset that he couldn't withdraw cash from his bank account during nonbanking hours, so he invented the now ever-present automated teller machine (ATM).[4]

To use dagnabbits to your advantage, start by thinking through, discussing, or observing your target audience (refer to your Creativity Brief) in action. Even better, interview people who are deeply embedded in your challenge (customers, colleagues, investors, and so on, depending on what creative problem you are working to solve). What are the natural pain points? Where do people get hung up? What bottlenecks exist? Find the dagnabbits, and you will quickly uncover a number of jumping-off points for creativity.

TDWR (Think, Doodle, Write, Repeat)

Advertising legend Ernie Perich likes to start his projects with a simple yet powerful approach: think, doodle, write, repeat (also known as TDWR).[5] Ernie loves to doodle and let his pencil lead the way down the path of creativity. A doodle—unlike a chart, diagram, or illustration—carries a whimsical, unfinished quality to it that makes it the ideal breeding ground for new ideas. A doodle is meant to be free-flowing and even sloppy.

Let your mind wander without limitations as you doodle ideas. Don't worry about your artistic ability—some of the best ideas began as stick figures. Many people learn and process things visually, so doodling away can help spark ideas. Spend an hour doing several cycles of TDWR in a free-flowing style. Don't edit, judge, plan, or even reread your doodles until the exercise is over. Be playful and let your mind and pen wander. The only rule should be that there are no rules.

Secrets of the Jazz Masters

Smoke-filled, late-night jazz clubs are hotbeds of spontaneous creativity, and creative sparks are the language of jazz. Like all great creative activities, jazz is intense, fluid, and high-energy. The following are five of the best jazz musician secrets, which you can use to unleash your own fresh thinking.

Trading Fours

There's a fun improvisational technique in which jazz musicians alternate short, four-measure solos, appropriately named "trading fours." This round-robin is separate from the longer, more involved solos of each of the musicians. Rather than one musician telling her story with her own extended solo, the group works together to tell a collective story by handing off the storytelling to the next musician every four measures. Each musician listens carefully so that she can build on the musical ideas of those who have played before her in the session.

This legendary jazz improvisation technique can be a powerful way for you to spark your own creativity. Instead of four measures of jazz melodies, you'll be trading ideas and concepts around your Creativity Challenge. Sit in a circle with your group and give it a try.

Start with a single creative spark. It could be anything from a vague thought to an image to a vision of the completed project. For example, suppose you're working on designing a new computer chip, and you start with "skiing in Aspen." From there, let the natural creativity of the group unfold and try to build on the initial idea while weaving back to your topic. The ski lifts could end up becoming an inspiration for a new type of vertical assembly line for your computer chips. Or the pattern made by skiers in the snow could be a new imprint architecture on the silicon. Trading fours has inspired jazz musicians and their audiences for seventy years, and can certainly help you spark your own imagination.

Building Contrast

One of the most engaging elements of a great jazz solo is contrast. Think how boring a trumpet solo would be if it were nothing but a string of the same notes played nonstop from beginning to end. Great solos develop and build, weaving in and out while telling an exciting story.

A jazz guitar solo may start slow and quiet, for example, and gradually build to a fast, loud peak. Once the peak has been reached, the solo may begin to retreat as if climbing down a mountain, until it ends in the same slow, quiet way it started. A bass solo may build tension with dissonant notes that make you squirm in your chair, then release that tension to create a feeling of calm groundedness. Often, contrast is the element that creates the most beautiful solos and the most appreciative audiences.

Great business improvisation is no different. Rather than groping for your creativity's on-off switch, fan the creative embers by exploring the contrasts of a simple, easy idea. For example, your Creativity Challenge may be to "increase the close rate of our sales team." Using contrast, you would first begin with an idea such as "provide better training to the salespeople." Playing around with that idea using contrasts may inspire thinking like this:

- **Vary training intensity.** Start with two weeks of intense training, then taper it down to three hours a month for six months, then bring the team back for another intensive weeklong workshop.
- **Alternate trainers.** For the first day, use a warm and nurturing trainer. Next, use a drill sergeant type who shakes the group up. End with a motivational trainer who pumps up the team to hit the market hard.
- **Combine multiple training tactics.** Break up each two-hour training session into four thirty-minute parts devoted to product knowledge, role-playing exercises, overcoming objections, and competitive insight.

Even if your initial spark is totally unrelated to the problem at hand (the best creativity often flows from random, unrelated concepts such as Italian dining, stamp collecting, or youth soccer), try using contrast to play around with the idea and see if you can solve your challenge in a nontraditional and more compelling way.

Mixing It Up

If you listen to a jazz group playing the same song every night for a month, you'll discover that it never sounds the same. For example, one night a group may play the classic jazz standard "All the Things You Are" in a medium-swing style. The next night it may be played in a smoking-fast bebop style, and the next as a slow and touching ballad. The group may play around with instrumentation, one night including the entire combo in a song, the next featuring only guitar and saxophone. Mixing it up not only keeps the music fresh for audiences but also keeps the musicians fresh with new ideas.

The same is true for you and your creative project. Mixing things up will help you bring exciting sparks to a cold start and drive fresh thinking throughout your creative endeavors. Here are some ways to mix it up:

- Use a different room for each brainstorming session
- Begin each session with a different warm-up exercise
- Change the order of your meeting agenda items frequently
- Conduct your meetings at different times of the day

You can also try mixing up your idea flow. For example, you may challenge the group to focus only on the very beginning of your creative project, and later challenge them to focus only on the ending. You could have the team generate small, incremental, safe ideas one day and the next day switch to giant, audacious, world-changing concepts. Maybe one day you generate ideas for a specific type of customer, and the next day you go for another target group. One session could focus on low-cost solutions and the next could focus on expensive ones. Mixing it up like jazz musicians can unlock hidden gems of creativity.

Leaning on the Masters

When studying the art of jazz, students not only learn technique but spend a significant portion of their time learning from the masters. Understanding how Dexter Gordon crafts his solos or how Sonny Rollins builds excitement or how Oscar Peterson uses the special technique of playing in unison octaves helps up-and-coming jazz musicians gain both perspective and inspiration. Studying the masters also helps aspiring musicians in three other ways: it provides a platform of context and history on which to build, offers a source of inspiration and ideas, and provides specific concepts that musicians can adapt into new musical challenges.

You can benefit your creativity greatly by looking to the techniques of masters of creativity and innovation—information you can find through any library or online search. How would Edison have approached your product design challenge? How did Einstein approach his research? What did Henry Ford do when he was stuck on a problem? Where did Picasso go when he needed a fresh perspective? How would Mark Zuckerberg (founder of Facebook) attack your new social media strategy?

I have a few riffs that I learned by studying jazz guitar virtuoso Wes Montgomery. Sometimes when I'm stuck in a solo, I will play these licks not only to regain my footing but also to spark ideas. Or I sometimes try McCoy Tyner's technique of "quartal harmony," an unusual and creative way of voicing chords, to open my mind to fresh possibilities.

To apply the age-old practice of leaning on the masters, try to discover some patterns or approaches that you can use as part of your overall creativity arsenal. Start small by learning one or two approaches from one legend in any field (business, art, science, politics, and so on) and see if you can apply those ideas to your own Creativity Challenge. As you continue to build your creativity muscles, you can keep adding to your repertoire, and before you know it, you'll be creating like the masters.

Substituting a Single Element

Great jazz musicians love to substitute one thing for another in a technique they call "subbing it out." Like a chef who decides to swap cilantro for basil in a recipe, jazz musicians find fresh ideas by substituting, for example, one chord, scale, or rhythmic pattern for another. By leaving other elements of the music exactly the same while making one surprising substitution, these musicians often ignite spectacular creative sparks.

You can use this same technique to generate sparks of inspiration in your work. Maybe you are working on a new type of packaging for your product. How could you revolutionize the design by leaving everything else alone and simply changing the way the package opens? Perhaps your Creativity Challenge is to streamline a twelve-step assembly line. Ask yourself how you might make the most improvement by changing only one of those twelve steps. If you are working on a TV commercial, what if you swapped out a male actor for a female one? Or replaced the classical background music with rock?

Playing with substitutions is a simple and powerful way to open up fresh perspectives and ideas. To get started, think about your Creativity Challenge (or even the status quo) as several unique and interconnected parts. Then simply take one part at a time and try swapping out something fresh. What if we swapped aluminum for plastic? What if we used contract labor instead of full-time employees? What if we sold our product directly instead of through distributors? Let your imagination run wild as you substitute ideas to unlock your creativity. And follow the jazz musician's lead when you try substitutions that don't work. If you really hit a clunker, just play it with confidence. "Wow, that piano player is really avant-garde!" "That idea is crazy!" "How creative!" Then keep trying new combinations. Soon you'll discover untapped resources of sparks and imagination.

Supporting the Combo

Jazz, this fluid, improvisational art form, is all about taking risks and trying new things. Going out on limb can be scary, but it is where the magic happens. Extending yourself outside your comfort zone is the way to discover the best rewards. But jazz is also about

Don't Fall into the Jazz Trap

The most in-demand jazz musicians are not typically the ones with the most blazing technique or dazzling solo ability. The ones who always find work are those who support the collective output, not the divas. What makes jazz performances memorable is not breathtaking speed or technique; the best jazz is all about establishing a connection and crafting true, artistic, musical expression. It's about creating something special that resonates with your audience.

The best leaders and the most valuable people in any organization aren't selfish, egocentric show-offs. I call that kind of behavior "the jazz trap" because I've seen it doom many musicians on the jazz stage. They get so caught up in a look-what-I-can-do mind-set that they lose connection with their audience. These musicians add complexity for the sake of it, and are so busy showing off their technical brilliance that their art suffers (as does anyone who happens to be listening). When you're leading a creative team, remember to avoid the jaws of the jazz trap. It can stop you dead in any field.

listening—to your fellow musicians, the audience, and your own creative voice.

Creative business leaders also succeed by listening—to their teams, customers, competitors, industries, and suppliers. Listening is key to spotting emerging trends, finding best practices, and developing your most creative ideas. Focused listening fosters adaptation, and results in group-driven solutions. Seeking inspiration and creativity from others enables you to adapt in real time to your own Creativity Challenge.

The new era of business rewards those who collaborate and work to serve their colleagues and their customers. Individual brilliance is great, but a tightly integrated group becomes unstoppable. As the African proverb states, "When spider webs unite, they tie up a lion."

Don't forget to keep your creativity directed toward solving your Creativity Challenge. Focus on finding the best—not the most complex—solutions. Let your creativity flow completely unrestricted throughout the creative process, but then select the solution that will create the best results, not the most dazzling display.

Jazz improvisation is like a fluid conversation among friends; you make it up as you go. There's no script, and the best discussions are never rehearsed. Think of yourself as a jazz musician, taking risks and using these techniques to improvise fresh and original ideas. Imagination will flow. Inspiration will hit. Sparks will ignite. And that blank page will be no match for your unbridled creativity.

Building Your Creativity Chops

This chapter is packed with games, activities, and ideas to ignite creative sparks and get ideas flowing. Here are some riffs on those ideas that can help you chart your creative course:

1. **Come up with the worst idea.** Consider the problem in front of you and then look for the worst solution—the idea that would achieve just the opposite of the result you're looking for. For example, instead of asking "How do we generate fewer customer complaints?" you might ask "How do we generate *more* complaints?" You can do this exercise with your group. Give each person two minutes to explain why his or her idea is horrible, then let the team discuss and choose the worst of all. In the process, see what new ideas you can uncover for improvement.

2. **Substitute it.** Think of one change you can make to an existing process or approach that impacts your Creativity Challenge, then imagine the ways that this single change might alter outcomes. Consider all the implications of that single change for the challenge you face, to see if it sparks ideas for a fresh approach.

9

●

Igniting the Sparks of Creativity

The Eight Most Powerful Techniques

I can't understand why people are frightened of new ideas.
I'm frightened of the old ones.

—JOHN CAGE

Jazz masters aren't alone in their search for multiple paths through the creative process. In the ancient military strategy book *A Book of Five Rings*, Japanese swordfighter Miyamoto Musahi advised to "Never have a favorite weapon." When it comes to generating great ideas, the same concept applies. Artists master different techniques. Great chefs can prepare meals in many styles. Venture capitalists understand dozens of different approaches to structuring their investments. The most effective warriors, jazz musicians, and business leaders have a variety of tools available to help them reach their objectives.

Having a broad arsenal of techniques enables people in all fields and disciplines to drive better results. Auto mechanics often proclaim the need to use the "right tool for the job." Mountain climbers will tell you that the right equipment can be the difference between life and death. When you tackle Creativity Challenges, you will need to draw on a full tool kit of techniques in order to find the most effective solutions. In Chapter Eight, you learned how to generate creative sparks. Here I'll offer a few proven techniques for igniting those sparks and stoking the flames of creativity—ideas that will open up multiple paths for you as you continue your journey of discovery. But first, let's take a minute to consider some guiding principles for the road ahead.

Check Your Left Brain at the Door

We've talked a bit about the difference between left-brain (analytical, logical, judgmental, linear) thinking and right-brain (free-flowing, creative, nonlinear) thinking. Because you probably spend most of your life in left-brain mode, those thought patterns are likely to be dominant and more well developed for you. During the idea generation process, you need to check your left brain at the door. This is easier said than done, because your highly developed left brain will want to jump in and contribute. Resist that diabolical temptation with all your being! Keep your left brain locked out of the room—it will only hamper your creative efforts. Don't worry—we'll reunite your left brain and right brain in the next chapter for some whole-brain thinking to sort the good ideas from the bad ones. There will be plenty of time to pacify that needy left brain and calm your nerves with thoughtful business analysis, measurement, action plans, scoring, and even metrics. In the meantime, give your right brain a chance to shine.

The Eight Commandments of Ideation

I call these the *Eight Commandments of Ideation,* but you can also consider them the Eight Commandments of Idea Ignition. Following these rules is critically important in bringing out a high quantity of high-quality ideas. The creative process, like the first sparks of a flame, must be supported, nurtured, and embraced wholeheartedly to generate the best results. By remembering these commandments, you'll protect and nurture your creative ideas and those of your team, and by doing so, establish a supportive framework for imagination and creativity:

1.   **Thou Shall Not Judge.** As ideas begin to flow, you must do everything in your power to *let them flow*. No person should be allowed to offer any judgment on any idea. The Ignite phase is about generating ideas, not ranking them. Just let the creative sparks burst forth. There will be plenty of time to evaluate them later.

2.   **Thou Shall Not Comment.** Even if the person next to you throws out the stupidest idea you've ever heard, let the process continue. Any negative comment or criticism will change the mood in the room, and the group will begin to clam up. Your commentary will distract the ideation process. Limit your reactions to a very short "wow," "cool," or "sweeeeeet."

3.   **Thou Shall Not Edit.** Don't let your inner editor join the session. At this point, it doesn't matter where the comma goes in the sentence or how to best word something. The font choice, color palette, and idea name are irrelevant. Editing is a left-brain activity and is a completely separate process than idea generation. Keep it that way. Let the ideas come out, sloppy and uninhibited. Later on, you'll have plenty of time to edit.

4.   **Thou Shall Not Execute.** The second an idea hits the whiteboard, you can easily become distracted by thinking about execution. You'll wonder how the idea will come to life. Who will run it? What will it cost? What does the project plan look like? What are the financial implications? Where will the work take place? When will we begin? These are great questions for later, but they will crush creative ideas and should be avoided like the plague at this stage in the process.

5.   **Thou Shall Not Worry.** As we've discussed throughout this book, fear is the single biggest blocker of creativity. Release fear in

order to unshackle your true creative potential. If you are leading the group, create an environment where people feel comfortable taking risks and have no fear of embarrassment or negative consequences. The best way to encourage this is to set an example. If you aren't afraid to toss out silly, outrageous ideas, you will set the stage for others to release their fears as well and let their most creative thinking come out.

6.   **Thou Shall Not Look Backwards.** Although we can learn a lot from the past, it can also handcuff our ability to reinvent the future. "We tried that six years ago and it didn't work out so well" is a highly limiting belief. Don't let the past inhibit your thinking. Every idea is new at this moment, and you and your team should share every one of them that you believe has merit.

7.   **Thou Shall Not Lose Focus.** Idea sessions can easily break down into wandering, so don't let your brainstorm energy get lured down another path toward a different Creativity Challenge or topic. When side issues arise, add them to your Parking Lot (introduced in Chapter Five). This keeps the group focused on the task at hand while still making sure that important concepts are discussed later.

8.   **Thou Shall Not Sap Energy.** There are two types of people in the world: Zappers and Sappers. When you are with a Zapper, you feel energized. You become engaged, you lean forward, you feel stimulated—the ideal state for creative expression. Then there are the Sappers. These are the folks who drain your energy with negativity and droning commentary that suck the life out of the room and kill creativity. Manage collective energy the same way you manage time or money. Ban BlackBerry-checking and clock-watching, and keep the energy up with high-fives, cheers, and positive vibes for all.

Print out a copy of these rules and tape them to the wall before any brainstorming session to make sure that you nurture the delicate and vital creative sparks of the group. Bring a bell, kazoo, drum, or other noisemaker to the session. Every time someone breaks one of the commandments, loudly ring the bell or beat the drum. Make your whole team responsible for enforcing these rules and holding each other accountable. Think of these eight commandments as nonnegotiable, and make sure everyone on your team agrees to them before any idea generation begins.

Ignite the Sparks!

I've scoured the world looking for the best techniques to ignite creativity. Here are eight of the most effective exercises to keep the excitement building during brainstorming sessions.

EdgeStorming

We've all heard of brainstorming. This technique is like brainstorming's rebellious cousin. The concept of EdgeStorming is to take your brainstormed ideas to the absolute extremes. It forces you to break through conventional wisdom, to go far beyond small incremental changes and connect with exaggerated thoughts. If ever there was a chance to be bold, this is it!

Cirque du Soleil EdgeStormed its way to unbelievable success. Instead of developing a slightly better circus and competing head-to-head with the market leader, one-hundred-year-old Barnum & Bailey Circus, its founder, Guy Laliberté, smashed conventional wisdom and dared to be remarkably different. He imagined a "dramatic mix of circus arts and street entertainment," a groundbreaking performance that encompassed incredible dance, cutting-edge stage design and lighting, breathtaking costumes, and unique venues. He wasn't interested in taking the old model and making it a little better. He went *all the way*.

The results, like their shows, are remarkable. Over the last twenty-five years, the company has grown to $1 billion in revenue and more than four thousand employees. They perform nineteen shows in 271 cities around the globe. The average ticket price for their sold-out shows is over three times more than the often half-empty Barnum & Bailey Circus.

To begin your own EdgeStorming session, conduct a normal brainstorming session where various people from the group toss out ideas, but ask the group to take each idea to its furthest possible extreme. To make the list, ideas must be outrageously big or small, loud or soft, expensive or cheap. By forcing yourself to the edges, you'll uncover countless fresh and new ideas. Of course, later you can always taper those ideas back to a more realistic stance, but EdgeStorming helps you see bold new possibilities where you otherwise may not—like the original 1966 *Star Trek* line, "To boldly go where no man [or woman] has gone before."

The Long List

This is a technique for developing fresh ideas that I first learned back in college, and still use today with great results. I was in a course about creating magazine and newspaper ads. The class was divided into teams, and we were assigned the task of developing headlines for a Florida State Lottery ad campaign. No problem, we thought, until the professor dropped the bomb. Each group was to return with no less than two hundred headline ideas. We had sixty minutes. Wowza!

When I've used the Long List technique with my organization's teams, it's never failed to generate ideas that push beyond boundaries. Here's how it typically goes. After the shock wears off, the team (or teams, if you prefer to form multiple smaller groups) begin generating ideas. The first ideas tend to be easy and obvious. Next come the edgy ones. Then the inappropriate ones. Then the gross ones and the bizarre ones and the stupid ones. We have to really dive deep and force ourselves to stretch our creative capacities to the limit. In most cases, our best ideas are clustered at the end of the list—they rarely come in at number 5, 11, or 19. Forcing yourself to generate a long list pushes your thinking and helps you discover your best work.

What was the winning tagline for the lottery ad campaign? "What will you say to your boss?"

To get the most from the Long List technique, follow these four simple steps.

1. **Articulate the objective.** To begin, make sure you have a very specific desired output. "Ideas for speeding up the second-shift production line at the Austin plant" is a better target than "increasing overall operational efficiency."

2. **Set your idea goal.** Next, set a time limit that forces you to generate a high volume of ideas without putting too much thought into each of them. The rate of two per minute is a good starting point. Examples of good Long List idea targets are one hundred ideas in fifty minutes or two hundred ideas in an afternoon.

3. **Do short bursts.** It is very difficult to stay in the creative zone for long periods of time, especially if you don't do it every day. You will see much better results by doing four fifteen-minute bursts with breaks in between instead of a full sixty minutes straight.

4. **Let it rip.** Remember, this is an exercise to get a high number of ideas out, which later on can be evaluated. Don't hold anything back. Make sure this is a fun, no-limits effort.

RoleStorming

We've talked about adopting different personas and role playing as a way to prepare for the creative process. RoleStorming takes this idea one step further, to help you develop your creative ideas without hampering them with too much left-brain editing or execution. In effect, you invite Steve Jobs to join your team.

Steve Jobs has the ability to envision the ultimate solution to a problem, with absolutely no regard whatsoever for the cost or executional challenges of how he'll actually get it done. As he broke new ground with the Apple II, Macintosh, iPod, and, more recently, the iPhone and iPad, he began by envisioning the ideal solution—the "what would it look like in a perfect world" concept. His gift is the ability to imagine breakthrough ideas without being distracted by the practicality of actually building them. If engineers, purchasing people, technicians, and designers tell him, "It can't be done," he demands that his ideas be brought to life. Even though he's had failures along the way (remember the Apple Lisa or the Apple Newton?), he has the guts to dream the impossible, and the fortitude to see those ideas through to fruition.

Although it may feel silly to you, the idea of RoleStorming is actually quite simple: save a seat for Steve Jobs at your brainstorming meeting. Literally. If you have a six-person team, it has now grown to seven because Steve Jobs has joined the group. Imagine that Steve is actually sitting there as you and your group launch the brainstorming process. In addition to each person contributing as himself or herself, have each person also suggest ideas on behalf of Steve Jobs. What would Steve do? How would he look at your Creativity Challenge? What ideal ideas might Steve have to create a transformational breakthrough?

The nice thing about this technique is that it removes the inhibitions of the team. Suggesting your own whacky idea may feel uncomfortable, but no one will mind if the idea comes from Steve. Steve suggests the ultimate solution to things, even if it is risky, expensive, and difficult to execute. You can't imagine him suggesting a small, minor product improvement or a tiny incremental change. Your virtual Steve Jobs can serve as a beacon of breakthrough creativity. He can be the big thinker in the room. (Of course, you and your team are actually the big thinkers, but it helps get the ideas flowing in a safe and fun way.)

If Steve Jobs is on vacation that day, invite Thomas Edison to your meeting. Or Quincy Jones. Or Barack Obama. Or Maya Angelou. Or someone from a different country (or planet). The key is to assign a specific persona and then have the team brainstorm ideas on behalf of that individual. To mix it up, you can also take turns actually acting as that person—for example, one of your team members actually pretends he or she is Steve Jobs for thirty minutes. It is a fun change of pace and can spur some great ideas. Don't forget the black turtleneck.

SCAMPER

Advertising legend Alex Osborn not only founded one of the most successful ad agencies in the world, BBDO, but also coined the phrase *brainstorming* and is credited for inventing the technique.[1] Later in his career, he invented another technique that is less well known but incredibly powerful: *SCAMPER*. This name is an acronym and stands for

Substitute
Combine
Adapt
Magnify or minimize
Put to other use
Eliminate
Rearrange or reverse

The SCAMPER technique can take you right back to the limitless creativity you had in kindergarten. Whether they're playing with blocks or playing dress-up or making a fort, children do these things naturally. They start with a concept and then try out different variations on the theme.

In Chapter Eight we discussed creative sparks. Try taking one of your new sparks and run it through SCAMPER thinking to build that idea into a raging inferno. For example, let's look at the world of breakfast cereal, which pretty much began with the Corn Flake (the creative spark). Here are some ways the SCAMPER technique is reflected in the product development efforts of some of the giants of that industry:

Substitute. Corn Flakes led to Bran Flakes (substitute ingredient). Puffed Rice helped launch Rice Krispies (substitute preparation). Substitutions can also include people, physical locations, production processes, flavors, and distribution channels.

Combine. Raisin Bran was born from combining bran flakes with raisins. What other combinations could you create? Cereal manufacturers are experts at this (Honey Nut Cheerios, Apple & Cinnamon Oatmeal). This step is about adding a new ingredient or combining two or more existing items into one.

Adapt. Are there things out in the world that you could adapt to your own Creativity Challenge? Cinnamon Toast Crunch came from borrowing the flavor of cinnamon toast and then adapting it into a cereal recipe. Take the all-American favorite of chocolate chip cookies, turn them into a cereal, and you have a winner: Cookie Crisp.

Magnify or minimize. Frosted Wheat became Frosted Mini Wheats. Granola evolved into low-fat granola. A regular box of Wheaties now comes in a giant, family-sized box.

Put to other use. Rice Krispie Treats are now packaged in separate units and sold as a competitor to the candy bar. Corn Flakes can be used in dozens of recipes, including breading for chicken and as an ingredient in stuffing. Of course, Kellogg's makes these recipes readily available and recommends the alternative uses.

Eliminate. Without nuts, reduced fat, sugar-free, only whole grains, and other banners are unavoidable as you walk down the cereal aisle at your local grocery store. Eliminating one or more aspects of an idea is a clever way to uncover brand new ideas.

Rearrange or reverse. Post launched Honey Bunches of Oats in 1989.[2] Today you can enjoy your Honey Bunches packaged with almonds, bananas, peaches, strawberries, chocolate clusters, cinnamon clusters, or vanilla clusters. What did Post do next? The company launched Just Bunches, eliminating the other elements of the cereal altogether. This playful approach helped the company build a cereal franchise around one original product idea.

The Opposite

We've talked about mixing it up, flipping problems, and finding the worst possible answers as ways to unleash creativity and spark creative ideas. To develop that same concept further, you can use The Opposite as a technique to take fresh ideas to a new level. Rather than solving the problem in front of you, what if you flipped the problem around? For example, instead of asking "How do we develop a product that every preteen girl will love?" you might ask "How do we create a product that all preteen girls will *hate*?" This type of thinking will lead to a fresh perspective and uncover some great new ideas. Zipcar is one organization that rewrote an industry by using The Opposite technique.

For years, the rental car business was stagnant. The top ten rental car companies were nearly indistinguishable. When one made a tiny change or improvement, the pack quickly followed. That veritable sea of sameness changed when Zipcar came along and launched the biggest revolution in the rental car business of the last thirty years.

Robin Chase, the company's founder, looked at how the typical competitors did business and then worked to do exactly the opposite.[3] Here are the important ways Zipcar used The Opposite in building its business model:

Typical Rental Car Company	Zipcar
Rent at airports	Rent in major cities
Rent by the day	Rent by the hour
Charge per day or week	Charge monthly membership fee
Sign out car via wait at counter	Use key fob to unlock cars directly
Pick up and return at company locations	Pick up and return in designated parking spaces right in cities

Line by line, Zipcar studied conventional wisdom and then had the courage to do the opposite. The results? Zipcar went from zero to $100 million of revenue in only four years, and has locations in over fifty cities and at more than a hundred college campuses. Growth and profitability have skyrocketed, while the old guard suffers with declines and losses. The Opposite certainly provided some zip for the customers, team members, and investors of this cool company.

As you approach your own Creativity Challenge, start by making a list of ideas, processes, or traditional techniques you can oppose. For example, make a list of all the ways you are currently approaching the problem or all the ways your competitors handle a situation or how the industry typically approaches a product offering. Or list all the things you've tried in the past that didn't work. When you have your list, identify the exact opposite approach for each item. If everyone else charges for delivery, for example, you would list "free delivery." If the traditional model calls for a certain solution, try suggesting the polar opposite. This oppositional thinking can help you generate fresh and inspiring ideas and will certainly help you break free from conventional wisdom.

The Reese's Peanut Butter Cup

Remember the old TV spots: "You got your peanut butter in my chocolate!" "No, you got your chocolate in my peanut butter!" "Delicious!" Two great tastes brought together to create something remarkable, as the slogan goes. Combining two distinct concepts to form an entirely new one is the root of the Reese's Peanut Butter Cup technique.

Think about some of the items you use every day, and you're likely to be able to trace them back to their origins: the combination of two or more distinct items or ideas. The SUV you drive is a combination of a car and a truck. The ubiquitous Snuggie is a combination of a blanket and a sweater. Your La-Z-Boy recliner, a combination of a bed and a chair. *American Idol* is a mix of talent show, live concert, and reality TV drama (character development, arguing judges, and so on).

The Reese's Peanut Butter Cup technique is the foundation of thousands of products, concepts, scientific advances, artistic endeavors, and even efficiency gains. Creativity Challenges of all sizes and shapes can be conquered using this framework.

To begin, list as many "ingredients" as possible. If you are working on a better way to deal with customer complaints, list all the current ways you handle the complaints along with all the other examples you can find from your industry and other industries. Maybe an unrelated field such as high-end hospitality does one thing while a fast-food burger joint does something very different. Once you have a long list of possible ingredients, try random combinations to see if you can get a better end result by combining two things that were previously unconnected.

To push your thinking even further, include random things or ideas on your list. In the previous example, what if you included a touch-screen kiosk? Or a gardening tool? Or a set of paintbrushes? Or a Broadway musical? Or Oprah Winfrey? You can go so far as to flip open a dictionary (remember those?) to a random page and grab any word that you stumble upon. It can't hurt to add them to the list. What you may discover is a completely unorthodox and refreshing approach to your Creativity Challenge, and new ideas that you would otherwise never have imagined.

The Blindfold

Throughout the book, we've discussed the importance of clearly articulating your Creativity Challenge and making sure everyone is working toward the same target. The more clarity the better. The Blindfold takes exactly the opposite approach. The technique involves keeping the people who participate in the creative process a little in the dark at first to break through any preconceived notions or biases.

Brian Gillespie, the chief creative officer for the San Francisco marketing agency BarCom, uses the Blindfold as one of his favorite techniques.[4] For example, let's say he had an assignment from P&G to develop a marketing campaign to encourage consumers to buy 2X Ultra Tide, which is at a premium price point to alternative detergents.

The traditional approach would be to clearly articulate the objective, discuss all the product attributes that make it cost more, and then finally to brainstorm advertising ideas. Brian prefers to mix it up. He'll keep the actual Creativity Challenge vague so that his team doesn't focus only on quickly reaching an easy outcome.

When the group assembles, they are not told the specific challenge or even the client name. Brian may begin the session, for example, by brainstorming around "How can Lexus charge a premium for its high-quality cars?" Then he might ask, "Why do consumers pay more for some products over others?" or "Which products do you use that you are willing to pay a little more for, and why?"

Brian finds that using the Blindfold helps generate some really original and nonobvious ideas. To use this technique, talk about a project and brainstorm *around* the topic without telling people what the project actually is or defining the desired outcome. It is akin to asking people to write a newspaper story without first revealing the headline.

Instinctively you may think that the Blindfold would hamstring the creative process, but instead it unleashes it. Your brain is an expert at recognizing patterns and repeating known connections. We were originally wired that way thousands of years ago to help us hunt and stay safe. The problem is that we can quickly jump to easy solutions and fail to stretch our creative capacity as a result of this hardwiring. The Blindfold helps break patterns, quick judgments, and biases to allow you and your team to forge entirely new ground.

Brain Writing

Collaboration can both help and hinder idea generation sessions. On the one hand, talented people can play off each other's ideas and build into a crescendo of brilliance. On the other hand, as we've seen in our discussion of groupthink and other examples, people's ideas can be negatively impacted by the group, and they sometimes end up withholding their creativity rather than letting it shine. In some cases, the entire group echoes the ideas of the most vocal or high-ranking people.

Brain Writing alleviates this issue. This technique helps avoid dominant personalities, fancy titles, and groupthink. In this exercise, each person writes an idea on a slip of paper and then places the idea in the center of the table. (You could also ask for more than one idea, such as three ideas in three minutes.) This act of isolated creativity helps avoid group influence. Once all the ideas are gathered, randomly select one from the pile and go around the table, with each person required to expand on the idea. Repeat this process until all the papers have been explored or you discover an absolutely killer idea.

University of Texas at Arlington has developed a Group Creativity Lab under the direction of Professor Paul Paulus.[5] In a fourteen-year study, Paulus staged and studied more than one thousand brainstorming sessions. What he discovered is that "Group brainstorm sessions often produce less and worse ideas than individual sessions because being in a group can be distracting." He discovered that Brain Writing can generate as much as 40 percent more ideas than individual sessions alone.

You can play around with variations of the Brain Writing technique. The Batelle Institute in Frankfurt, for example, developed a technique called Successive Integration.[6] In this method, each person writes an idea. Then, starting with one person's idea, the paper is passed to the next person in the group, who must read it out loud and then add to it. Each idea gains momentum as it is passed around the group and built upon. Once the group feels that an idea is fully developed, they move to the next person's written idea and repeat the exercise. This technique is powerful in that it involves both individual (written ideas) and group (passing around, expanding) creativity.

Another variation you might try is called the Stepladder, developed by Steven Rogelberg, Janet Barnes-Farrell, and Charles Lowe in 1992.[7] This framework manages how members enter the decision-making group and encourages all members to contribute on an individual basis *before* being influenced by anyone else. The Stepladder results in a wider variety of ideas and prevents people from "hiding" within the group. It also helps people avoid being "stepped on" or overpowered by stronger, louder group members. Here's how it works. Start with a core group of two and brainstorm ideas around your Creativity Challenge. From there, introduce new members to the group one at a time. Each new member who enters the group must share his or her new ideas before the core group shares theirs.

Whatever variation you use, Brain Writing is an important technique for generating ideas and then pushing them to the next level. In addition to fending off the creativity-killing power of groupthink, Brain Writing enables your team to nurture the creative sparks of their ideas and gives them a chance to ignite into something truly amazing.

The Power of the Group

There is a famous psychology experiment in which a professor draws a line on the board that is around twelve inches long. He then asks the class to raise their hands and estimate how long the line is. The professor first calls on three or four "plants," people who are in on the experiment. "About 3.5 feet," the first person says. "Hmmm... maybe 2.75 feet," the next person guesses. "I'd say just short of 4 feet," declares the third. Next, the professor begins to call on other students not in on the experiment. The benchmark set by the first three students influences the remaining students, who give answers that are closer to the biased responses. Students do begin to guess shorter lengths, but the average guess still ends up well in excess of two feet. In a control group without the "plants," students accurately determine the length, with the average guess correctly right around one foot. This classic experiment illustrates the power of the group and how a few vocal members can lead groups astray.

Are You Ready for Lift-Off?

As you approach the idea generation process, you may want to try several of these techniques over the course of a few different sessions. You should try alternating between group and individual sessions, and change up the venue, time of day, and approach in order to generate the most compelling ideas. Just remember the purpose behind these powerful techniques: you're trying to fan the flames of your creativity—to feed those tiny creative sparks until they become an explosion of ideas.

When the space shuttle lifts off, it burns 65 percent of its fuel in the first twenty minutes of a two-week flight; that's because it has to overcome a massive gravitational pull to reach orbit. Like the space shuttle, your ideas have to break through some natural bonds of resistance. Getting started is the hardest part. You could spend your whole life preparing, analyzing, and covering your tracks. Or you can move forward with the spirit of a warrior. Leap into your work and imagine you are Van Gogh, da Vinci, or Mozart. You have the same talents inside you, and now you have some specific techniques to fill the canvas with your own inspired creativity.

Building Your Creativity Chops

You've learned eight powerful techniques for igniting fresh, creative ideas. Use the following riffs on those techniques to throw gasoline on your creative fire:

1. **RoleStorm!** Think about a favorite character in a book or movie. It could be the infamous Gordon Gekko from *Wall Street*, the savvy and sophisticated James Bond, or even the shy and inquisitive Edward Scissorhands. Spend a couple minutes getting into character. How does he or she speak, think, and behave? Next, take on your chosen persona as you brainstorm fresh ideas to conquer your Creative Challenge. Let the ideas flow, coming from *the character* instead of you.

See what Superman or Lex Luthor might come up with to help solve your next pressing business challenge.

2. **Chocolate meets peanut butter.** To begin, set a timer for five minutes. Next, have everyone on your team brainstorm how many things they can think of in the world that are a Reese's Peanut Butter Cup—in other words, products, services, or ideas that are the combination of two or more existing things. For example, sailing, parachutes, and waterskiing were combined to create parasailing. Give each person a point who can identify a real-world example of his or her own and award a small prize for the individual who comes up with the most. After five minutes of mental exploration, you and your team will be ready to jump-start some new ideas of your own. Immediately following this exercise, apply the Reese's Peanut Butter brainstorming technique to your own Creative Challenge and let those delicious new ideas fly.

LAUNCH

10

•

Bringing Your Ideas to Life

The Launch

Man who says it cannot be done should not interrupt man doing it.
—CHINESE PROVERB

Now that your whiteboards are filled with ideas, it's time to choose the best ones and put them into action. Great ideas are worthless unless they are brought to life. But how do you sort the good from the bad? How do you determine which ones to back and which ones to toss? How do you define success and measure the value you've created? Welcome to step 5 of the Disciplined Dreaming Process: *Launch.*

This phase of the process calls for a return to whole-brain thinking: reuniting your left-brain strengths with those of your right brain. It's time to bring back some business rigor to help launch your creative ideas—to take them from the proverbial back of the napkin into reality. As your ideas come to life, you'll get to enjoy the benefits of your creativity—for your company, your customers, your industry, and your career.

With both sides of your brain in full force, you begin the task of finding the best among the long list of ideas you've created. It is time to switch from idea generation mode to idea selection mode, and then into idea execution mode. The first thing you'll want to come to terms with is that you can't bring every idea you generated to life. Some of the best concepts in business history were selected at a ratio of one keeper to one hundred "passes." The important thing is to accept that it's okay to let go of ideas, even if you think they are strong. Make sure to save them, of course, as you may want to bring them to life at a later date.

In this chapter, we'll explore a number of frameworks and techniques that will help you winnow down your list, pick the best ideas, and then put them into action. We'll begin with a more traditional approach, and then move into unorthodox methods to launch your ideas and solve your Creativity Challenge.

Selecting Your Best Ideas

You've come up with a range of good ideas, and now it's time to select the best of them. The following sections offer techniques for narrowing down your choices to a single, best idea.

Scoring Your Ideas: The Matrix

The most common approach to idea selection is the Matrix Scoring technique. This is a classic business school concept, but don't hold that against it. It's still a powerful technique and can help you not only choose your best ideas but also sell your ideas to outside stakeholders. Using it, you will take a handful of your best ideas and score them on several factors that are most important to you. You'll then add up the total scores.

For example, let's say you work for Dell, and your Creativity Challenge is to develop a way to speed up the production process for building laptop computers. You would list the various ideas you had on the top of a simple spreadsheet, and list the things that are important to you on the side. From there, you would fill in the matrix, scoring each item on a 1–10 scale (with 10 being the highest).

Here's an example of a completed matrix:

	Hire More Workers	Install New Factory Equipment	Simplify Customer Choices	Use Robotics and Automation
Time savings	6	8	7	9
Low initial investment	8	4	8	2
Easy to implement	7	4	6	5
Requires little training	7	5	8	9
Fast change timeline	9	5	8	6
Low safety hazards	3	9	9	10
Low ongoing costs	1	8	8	10
Low operation risk	8	7	2	9
Long-term benefit	1	8	2	10
TOTAL SCORE:	**50**	**58**	**58**	**70**

In this example, you can see that the robotics and automation idea carries the highest score. The Matrix Scoring approach helps you compare multiple factors on an apples-to-apples basis and quantify elements that may be subjective.

The scores from this technique should *guide* your decision-making process, not determine it. After further discussion, your group may decide that new factory equipment is a better choice for your company. Use the numbers to support your judgment; you aren't subject to them.

The Poker Chip Method

As we've seen, the ideas of the highest-ranking people in the room can often dominate brainstorming sessions. You definitely don't want that syndrome to take over when you're selecting the one great idea your team will pursue. To avoid the influence of hierarchy or dominant team members in the idea selection process, try using the

Flying the Plane

In aviation, a pilot uses two methods to fly a plane: instrument flying rules (IFR) and visual flying rules (VFR). Skilled pilots are supposed to use the technical systems and gauges along with their own sight and judgment.

Imagine a pilot approaching a landing strip on a clear day. She sees the strip two hundred feet below, but the instruments indicate that her altitude is five thousand feet. You'd expect the pilot to use judgment to land safely rather than blindly follow the gauges and crash the plane into the ground.

But how often in the business world do we experience just the opposite?

We use complex models, historical data, and buzzwords like "key performance indicators" and "balanced scorecards." Like dashboard instruments, these tools are great, but they're not the one-and-only factor in creating success. We hire team members for their judgment and creativity, but often relegate them to merely following systems mechanically.

At your company, how many times have you run into a policy roadblock that inhibits your performance rather than assists it? You explain in vain that you want to take a different approach, only to be shot down because it is "not our policy." Flying on instruments alone is a surefire way to crash the plane and lose your most precious assets (employees, customers, culture, creativity).

What would happen at your company if "policies" became "guidelines"? What if we trusted talented team members to use their own experience and insight to do the right thing? The companies that fly on both IFR and VFR will win in the next era of business, the Age of Creativity.

Poker Chip Method. In this case, every team member in the room receives ten poker chips (you can use pennies if no poker chips are handy). Write your top few ideas on separate sheets of paper and spread them out across the table. From there, each person gets to "vote" with his ten poker chips. A person could spread his chips over his favorite three ideas, for example. Or someone could "bet the farm" and put all her chips on her single favorite idea.

The Poker Chip Method is helpful to get a quick, unfiltered, overall sense of what the team is feeling. If you as the leader were favoring one idea, but other ideas received many more votes, you may want to either reconsider your choice or at least realize that you a have a lot of work ahead of you to secure the full buy-in and support of the team. Taking an accurate temperature of your team can also help narrow the field of possibilities by eliminating ideas that may be cool but receive zero votes.

Trial by Jury

We've all grown up watching court shows on TV. *Perry Mason* paved the way for *LA Law, Matlock, Law & Order,* and *Boston Legal*. Although most of us didn't attend law school, we can all picture how a courtroom works. Each side presents its case to the jury, who renders a verdict after the evidence and arguments are presented. The same approach can help you lock in your best ideas by using the Trial by Jury.

1. Choose one person to represent each idea that you are seriously considering. Give that person a specific amount of time to prepare. (Depending on the complexity of the idea, this time frame could range from thirty minutes to a couple of weeks.)
2. Assemble a group of people (or even the whole rest of the team) to play the role of the jury.
3. Have one person make a timed opening argument. Ten minutes is a good starting point, but this can vary depending on the scope of the idea.
4. The person who will be presenting another idea (think of him as "opposing counsel") then gets a timed period to refute the concept, poke holes in the theory, and even cross-examine the original presenter. The time limit should be no longer than the original presentation.
5. Using the same rules and timing, now switch sides and have the second person make his own opening argument, followed by a counterargument period by the first presenter.

6.   After all competing ideas have been argued, give each presenter a timed period for closing arguments to sum things up and drive home her key points. Suggested length: approximately five minutes per person.

7.   Now it's the jury's turn to deliberate. Allocate a set amount of time (I'd suggest thirty minutes if you are following the example of ten-minute arguments). Elect a "foreperson" to then come back and render the verdict.

The Trial by Jury can be tremendous fun, while also providing a structured forum to debate the merits of competing ideas. All sides get equal time, and this system is designed to let the best idea win.

Value Mapping

A Matrix Scoring framework is a traditional way to select an idea. Now let's explore a fun alternative that can be equally powerful in choosing the right idea to pursue—Value Mapping. Instead of scoring ideas against such traditional factors as feasibility, time to market, anticipated return on investment, and risk, you use a set of values that are important to you and your company. As an example, the folks at the board game maker Cranium created their own word: CHIFF (clever, high quality, innovative, friendly, and fun).[1] When they set out to evaluate ideas, a big deciding factor is how well the idea meets the CHIFF profile. They use the CHIFF benchmark when hiring and evaluating team members, deciding on which markets to enter, and how to market their products. They are using the benchmark of *who they are* to guide decision making.

Leaders at Virgin, the parent company of Virgin Records, Virgin Books, Virgin Airways, and now Virgin Galactic (space travel) are willing to consider entering just about any new business as long as it meets their values criteria.[2] To be considered, a concept must

- Challenge existing rules
- Provide a better consumer experience
- Be more fun
- "Put a thumb in the eye of the complacent incumbents"

Rather than using a numerical score, the team at Virgin let their values dictate their actions. To Virgin, the spreadsheet matters less than the opportunity to "stick it to the man." Virgin is irreverent and edgy, funny and clever, youthful and energetic. Although the company's product offerings span several industries, its overall brand and attitude are totally consistent. Virgin's leaders are more likely to move forward with an idea if they think they can expand their message and calling as opposed to simply making a quick buck. They realize that their overall shareholder value is based on the growth and consistency of their brand and their values.

Another example of Value Mapping is asking if an idea is "NAF"—novel, attractive, and feasible. These are general terms that allow you to map your own values to the situation. In other words, how attractive is the opportunity to *you*? To some companies, "attractive" might be defined as high-growth, whereas others might define it as low-risk. Try putting your leading ideas through the NAF filter to see which ones emerge as front runners.

Many companies have specific innovation metrics. These goals may include a specific number of new product launches per year, a certain percentage of revenue from new services, or a set amount of cost savings through engineering efficiencies. If your company has specific goals tied to creativity, you can use them as a helpful tool in sorting out which ideas to pursue. You may be wrestling between two great ideas, but find one much more appealing after benchmarking them both against your company's innovation goals. Once again, you are using Value Mapping to help you align your ideas to your company's big-picture values and goals.

The Creativity Scorecard

In Chapter Three, I introduced you to the Creativity Brief, your North Star throughout the Disciplined Dreaming process. You began your creative process by creating that document, and now is the time to link back to it as you evaluate your ideas and launch the best ones into reality.

Score each idea you are considering on a 1–10 scale (with 10 being the highest) on a few key elements of the Creativity Brief. The purpose here is to see which ideas align best with your original objectives.

Here is an easy-to-use scorecard that links back to specific questions from the Creativity Brief:

Creativity Scorecard

	Idea 1	Idea 2	Idea 3	Idea 4
Does this idea meet your desired outcome?				
Does this idea solve your original problem?				
How strong of an impact will this idea make on your company and your career?				
How well will the idea be received by your target audience?				
Does the idea meet your written definition of success?				
How strong is the return on investment?				

Don't base your decisions only on this score. Instead, use it as a piece of valuable information that you should consider as one of several deciding factors. Apply your judgment, instinct, and experience to this score as well as the results of several of the other methods we've looked at.

Testing Your Selections

As you evaluate your list of ideas, you may find some that sound great in theory but quickly burn apart as they enter the atmosphere of reality. Billions of dollars are lost every year by companies moving forward with ideas that make sense in an ivory tower, but have significant practical or customer-related flaws. Now it's time to test-drive the idea or ideas you've chosen to pursue. By testing your ideas before fully implementing them, you have an opportunity to save the time, money, and frustration that can result from pursuing a flawed idea.

Prototyping

Prototyping is a powerful way to carefully examine ideas and begin to assess their real-world potential. Prototyping need not involve complex machinery or big investment. In fact, Play-Doh is one of my favorite "rapid prototyping" tools. Computer modeling is also an easy and low-cost way to sort the good ideas from the bad. No matter how crude, anything you can do to bring your idea to life so that you can examine it in a 3D format will help you determine whether it should receive further support or you should move on to the next one.

What about when the idea involves a service? Or experience? Or people? Role playing is the ideal technique to help determine which ideas make the most sense and to identify any "soft spots" that may exist. Simply act out the customer experience or service you are proposing. The more realistic the better. Costumes, accents, physical movement, location, and even temperature all play into a successful role play. The closer you can get to simulating the actual experience you are proposing, the more accurate your read on reality will be.

Let's explore these powerful prototype formats in more detail.

Physical Model This is what probably jumps to your mind when you first hear the word "prototype." Car companies have been building prototypes for years, ranging from small models of new ideas to full-scale concept cars. If your Creativity Challenge involves something physical, such as a new product, piece of equipment, or part, creating a prototype is a must-do. When it comes to evaluation, an idea written on a whiteboard is no match for a 3D physical model.

Product companies like Apple Computer and IKEA live and die by the prototype. Some of the most popular products evolve from literally thousands of physical prototypes, testing everything from usability to design to weight to "human factors." These models not only help determine whether or not a product should go forward but also aid in making adjustments, such as in the selection of materials, colors, and packaging.

Don't worry if you lack access to a rapid prototyping facility or the resources to build fancy models. Sometimes even crude prototypes do the trick just fine. Clay, inexpensive materials from a hardware store, or even remnants from a junkyard can help you bring a concept into the real world for further assessment.

Acting It Out If your Creativity Challenge involves a service (for either an external or internal customer), doing a role play is an ideal way to evaluate your ideas. You can also act out user sessions with physical models, simulations, and other media for any size or type of Creativity Challenge.

For example, maybe you've designed a new type of life insurance product and are considering whether you should formalize the service and bring it to market. Have one person from your group play the role of the salesperson and another play the role of a potential customer. Act out the sales call, having the potential customer issue several objections to the product while the salesperson has to describe the new product and articulate its benefits. In addition to having the rest of the group observe the session, try videotaping it. This will allow you to go back and review it at a later point, as well as compare this session with those of competing ideas.

Simulation The Edward Levy Company is about as old-line as you can get.[3] It removes and reuses sludge (manufacturing waste) from factories and has been doing it since the days of Henry Ford. But the company's president, Evan Weiner, is one of the most progressive and thoughtful leaders I've met. One of Evan's favorite techniques to use when evaluating ideas is simulation. He uses advanced software simulations of new manufacturing techniques as well as inner-office improvements and business modeling, and credits this technique for driving a significant impact on the company's bottom line.

By simulating an idea, you are able not only to see it in action but also to observe *how* it works. The simulation results may suggest tweaks or improvements to various elements of your idea. It is much easier to refine during a simulation than in the real world, where dollars, safety, and time can all be at stake. The military regularly uses simulations for combat drills in which lives are on the line. It's much better to experiment and get it right on a computer screen or on a simulation model than in the streets of Bagdad or the caves of Afghanistan.

Your approach to simulation will depend on your specific circumstances, but there is an abundance of simulation software applications readily available. You can also do simulations that are low-tech, with crude materials and basic supplies. If you are working to improve the flow of flight landings at a crowded airport, use model planes, paper runways, and a stopwatch. If you working on a new interface for an e-commerce store, build the bare-bones new functionality you want to test and have others use the new idea to simulate what a customer might experience.

Making a Film, Song, Painting or Story What better way to bring your ideas to life than to inject some art into the mix? You don't have to be a gifted filmmaker or singer to have your ideas take form in an artistic way. In fact, the "home-grown" style is often more real and more compelling. Here are some ideas that you can try out to prototype your ideas in various media:

- Draw a scene of your idea in use by stick figures.
- Using a low-cost video camera such as a Flip camera, make a one- or two-minute pitch for your ideas in the format of a movie trailer.
- Create a rap song about your idea.
- Write a short children's story about your idea. This method is not only fun but also helps you communicate your idea with clarity and simplicity.
- Film a series of interviews with random people explaining the merits of your idea. (Coworkers, people on the street, and your kids are all fair game.)
- Use finger paints to create a diagram or painting of your idea.
- Make your idea into a poem, limerick, or haiku.
- Create lyrics about your idea and sing them to a famous melody, such as "I've Been Working on the Railroad" or "Oh, Susanna."
- Make a video of happy customers using your new product, or of excited investors enjoying giant returns from your new cost-saving measures.

- Write a letter from the chairman of your company, dated one year in the future, explaining why your idea was such an enormous success.

These whimsical and nontraditional ways to bring your idea to life will push your creativity and help you connect with your ideas at a much deeper level. From there, you can start to deconstruct them and sort the good from the bad. Certainly you won't select an idea based on which had a better song, but the process of writing a song about an idea will help you determine if it is a keeper or not.

Demos When celebrity chef Rachael Ray conducts her show, she gets you excited about her recipes via demonstration. The act of preparing and then delivering a demo can help you better connect with your best ideas, while allowing an impartial audience to compare one idea to another.

In Silicon Valley, there is a seasonal ritual called Demo Days. These are events in which eager entrepreneurs present their ideas in rapid succession in order to attract the attention of venture capitalists interested in making investments. Each demo is less than five minutes long, requiring the entrepreneur to be concise and make every second count. Even with such limited time, the bulk of each presentation is in the form of a demonstration. The bright-eyed entrepreneurs don't just talk about their hot new technology: they *show it* through demonstration. The better the demo, the more likely the young company will be to catch the eye of an investor.

This same concept holds true for you. A great way to prototype your idea is to perform a demonstration. If you have competing ideas, allocate equal time and prepare a demonstration for each idea. In other words, conduct your own version of Demo Days for your team, your boss, or even your customers. Seeing how a product, service, or solution works in action is a great way to determine whether or not it deserves further investment and attention.

Mach 10 Innovation

New product development at ePrize used to follow the traditional approach: come up with a cool new product idea, spend a couple months and a bunch of money building it, then take it to market to see how it sells. Lots of up-front investment of capital and time, and a big risk to see how the market will respond.

In 2008, we flipped our innovation cycle upside down. We went from Idea → Development → Sales to a new model: Idea → Sales → Development. In the new model, we continued to brainstorm dozens of new product ideas. Instead of betting on (and investing in) one idea at a time, we began to move forward with as many as ten per month, but we built nothing more than a marketing sheet and a technical specification. We generated a much higher volume of ideas and brought them to market immediately, before the technical software was completed. From there, we let the customers vote with their wallets. Only when an idea was purchased by a real customer would we go forward with technical development.

I called this new model Mach 10 innovation, and it was hugely beneficial to both our clients and our company. From the clients' standpoint, they had dramatically more choices of fresh new ideas each month, and took advantage of our best thinking. From ePrize's standpoint, we significantly lowered our up-front development costs because we built only products that had been ordered. Giving the client more choices also drove revenue: several million dollars of Mach 10 ideas were sold within the first twelve months of the program. We were able to better serve our customers, invent more new products, and increase revenue simultaneously.

The core of the Mach 10 strategy is to bring products and services to customers early. Where old innovation models were based on internal testing and focus groups, Mach 10 brings live customers into the mix much sooner. It moves the testing process from the lab into the real world, offering a much broader array of choices in the market.

Another good example of Mach 10 innovation comes from Zara, the Spanish clothing retailer.[4] Experimentation and adaptation are truly part of the company's DNA. The process begins with store managers sending customer feedback and observations to in-house design teams via mobile devices. This helps the company immediately spot fashion trends and adapt merchandise to local tastes. Just-in-time production (an idea borrowed from the automotive industry) then gives the company an edge in terms of speed and flexibility. The result is a three-week turnaround time for new products (the industry average is nine months) and ten thousand new designs every year—none of which stays in stores for more than four weeks.

Internet ad campaigns now run in a similar fashion. Traditional advertising placed big bets on a single ad. After the campaign was launched, marketers relied more on religion (prayer) than science to ensure that their work was successful. Today's online marketing campaigns, in contrast, are incredibly sophisticated, automated, and data-driven. An advertiser today may launch a hundred different variations of an online ad to begin the campaign. Through advanced software and monitoring, ad-serving systems then begin to optimize which ads are working in which places. For example, ad 47 may out-perform ad 48 in sports-related media, such as ESPN.com or Yahoo Sports. Once this trend has been established, the system then delivers a much higher number of ad 47s to drive better performance. The system may also determine that ad 81 is getting an excellent response among thirty- to forty-five-year-old women. Accordingly, when the system identifies a Web user as part of this category, ad 81 it is. The mantra of the online ad world is "test and fail quickly."

Test ideas in the real world, immediately discard those that fail, then put your weight behind those that work.

Market-based feedback and testing can be very powerful for you. When you are winnowing down the list of ideas for your Creativity Challenge, explore the concept of taking several of the best ideas to market and letting the market (your customers), not you and your team, determine the best ideas. This helps avoid any biases from your group and gives you a much higher degree of accuracy: instead of guessing which idea will work the best, you are actually seeing which ones your audience will embrace.

Setting Your Metrics: Measurement

Once you've narrowed the field to one or two of your best ideas to pursue, you should think about how you plan to measure them. Solid metrics will help you not only determine the success of your idea as it relates to your Creativity Challenge but also secure necessary buy-in from others (bosses, investors, the board of directors, partners, suppliers, and so on). Zeroing in on key metrics and measuring against them as your idea comes to life will also help you refine the idea as it evolves.

In professional sporting events like basketball or football, there is always a real-time scoreboard that indicates the score along with other key metrics, such as time remaining, number of time-outs taken, which period is currently in play, or how many yards are needed for a first down. This real-time information not only helps the fans enjoy the game but also is vital to the coaches and players as they adapt their strategy on the fly. The same is true as you launch your creative idea. Having up-to-the-minute information will allow you to adjust your strategy so as to optimize the impact of your work.

To get started, create your own "Jumbotron" (the large scoreboards that you see in professional sports arenas). Your scoreboard doesn't have to cost millions; it simply has to clearly display the most important metrics so that you and your team can constantly monitor progress. Your scoreboard can be as simple as a large whiteboard that you update with daily stats or a poster board with flip numbers. At ePrize, we have plasma TVs mounted on the walls throughout our offices to make sure everyone in the company always knows the score. The plasmas display real-time information, such as up-to-the-minute sales numbers, quality metrics, utilization rates, and client satisfaction. In true ePrize spirit, the readouts are colorful, fun, and engaging. (Who said numbers have to be dry and boring?) Making sure our team always knows the score allows us to focus our efforts on a common result and also to course-correct, adapting our work in real time if something gets off track.

In your case, select the top key metrics that you plan to measure and track as your creative project moves forward. Warning: don't choose too many metrics to monitor, or you will quickly lose focus. Sports like baseball have literally thousands of metrics on each player and team, but Jumbotron scoreboards show only the most important five to eight key metrics. You need to do the same, or you will experience information overload. It will be impossible to process, understand, and adapt to ten or twenty or fifty metrics at a time. Narrow the field to a handful of the most important data points and stay focused on those.

If you are working to improve a manufacturing process, for example, your key metrics may include specific measures on throughput, production speed, quality, and safety. It is important to quantify all measures so that you and your team can understand and improve results. Scoring "quality," for example, is too subjective. One person may rate something's quality as good, while another thinks it's bad. Remove the subjectivity from your scoring wherever possible.

In this case, quality could be measured as the number of defects per thousand units or the percentage of products that clear quality control.

Every Creativity Challenge, big or small, should have key metrics of success. If you are working on a marketing campaign, key metrics may include the number of inbound inquiries, closing rates of salespeople, repeat business from existing customers, increases in revenue or order size, and decreases in customer attrition. If your Creativity Challenge is to launch a new online service, key metrics may include the number of new subscribers, average length of stay on your site per visit, referral rates of members inviting other members to join, and retention rates.

These are the important measurement takeaways:

- Clearly define a small number of key metrics
- Quantify and standardize your metrics so that they are consistent
- Align your team and other stakeholders (bosses, partners, and so on) around the same key metrics
- Create a scoreboard so that you and your team can constantly monitor results
- Use the insight gained from closely monitoring your key metrics to adjust and adapt your idea in order to maximize results

Building Your Action Plan

You've finally made it to the exciting point of launch. You and your idea are about to blast off, and you'll soon be enjoying the benefits of your creativity. There are hundreds of books on project planning and execution, so I won't go too deep on this topic. However, it is critical that you build a detailed execution plan to ensure that your great idea doesn't explode on takeoff.

Make sure that you've covered the basics, including

- Budget, forecast, and anticipated return-on-investment model
- Roles and responsibilities of team members during the execution phase
- Detailed timeline with clear milestones and checkpoints
- List of the top risks, and contingency plans if they occur
- Resources needed (money, people, time, equipment, facilities, travel, and so on)
- Communication and rollout plan

Taking Care of Business

You've gone through the Disciplined Dreaming creative process: you identified your Creativity Challenge; awakened your curiosity; raised your level of awareness; prepared your mind, culture, and environment; discovered creativity where it hides; generated creative sparks; ignited fresh ideas through powerful brainstorming techniques; selected the best ideas; established key measurements; and now are ready to release your best creative idea into the world. It is time to gracefully transition back into your normal business processes. You'll need to integrate your idea back into your own systems, as most ideas will not live in isolation but as part of a larger organization or community.

Move forward with boldness and thoughtfulness, with urgency and passion, and with a renewed sense of purpose and wonder. Congratulations! You have created and implemented a fresh, new idea. Whether it is big or small, you have made a difference. In some way, you have changed the world.

EPILOGUE

———●———

The Power of One

One of the most important concepts that I hope to have imparted to you in this book is the Power of One. It takes only one fresh idea, big or small, to make a difference. And that one idea is inside you right now, waiting to come out and come to life.

One idea.

One idea is all it takes to change your career.

One idea is all it takes to change your company.

One idea is all it takes to change your region.

One idea is all it takes to change our country.

And one idea is all it takes to change the world. In fact, one idea is the only thing that ever has.

So now it's your turn. Take the tools and concepts you've learned, and tap into your own brilliant creativity. That one idea is inside you right now. You have everything you need to seize it. Now it's your turn . . . to let your best creative ideas come out to play.

APPENDIX A

●

The Top Six Creativity Myths (and Truths)

Through my experience and research, I have identified six common myths that inhibit creativity. The good news is that each of them can be conquered and removed forever. Once you break free from these shackles, you will enjoy an overwhelming sense of freedom and your creativity will soar.

MYTH 1: Creativity is only needed at the top.

TRUTH: In today's business environment, creativity applies to everyone.

The companies that will win in this post-recession new world will have creativity as part of their DNA. You may think, "Creativity doesn't apply to me. It is only needed for CEOs, inventors, R&D teams, and artists." That may have been true fifty years ago in the Industrial Age, but today, creativity is everyone's job. It's *your* job.

Everyday Creativity applies in nearly all business situations. Breakthrough, game-changing innovations may not happen every day, but questioning the status quo and discovering better ways of serving customers and doing your job should be continuous activities.

MYTH 2: People are creative (or not) depending on their job or role.

TRUTH: Your role has nothing to do with your creativity.

Too often, people rank themselves low on creativity assessment tests because they are not good at painting, music, or theater. They create an artificial link between fields known for creativity and their own creative capacity. Being creative does not require you to be a talented saxophone player, a brilliant sculptor, or an inspiring dramatic actor. Creativity is something that all humans possess, in the same way that all humans breathe oxygen and drink water. Don't let labels dictate or limit your creativity.

MYTH 3: Creativity is "born"; it can't be developed.

TRUTH: Yes, it absolutely can.

In fact, we all have tremendous creative capacity as human beings. We just need to develop it. There is an overwhelming amount of scientific research confirming that you can grow your creativity at any age. This doesn't mean creativity is easy. Like any other pursuit, reaching your full creative potential takes time, energy, commitment, and hard work. The key point here is that creative potential is not predetermined, but rather a skill that is largely within your control to develop.

MYTH 4: Creativity isn't my responsibility.

TRUTH: Today, creativity is everyone's responsibility.

There isn't a job function that can't benefit from creative problem solving, fresh ideas for the future, or simply finding a better way.

MYTH 5: Creativity can't be managed or harnessed.

TRUTH: Developing creativity is the primary role you will play as a leader in the twenty-first-century business world.

Although businesses have processes for just about everything, no such process previously existed for nurturing creativity. The Disciplined Dreaming process will help you connect with your creative potential and lead your team's creativity, regardless of your title. Your success will be determined by your ability to provide a fertile environment for your team members, enabling them to express their creativity and imagination. The leadership role is radically shifting from a command-and-control emphasis to one of nurturing and supporting creative thinking.

MYTH 6: My technical skills and experience are enough.

TRUTH: Creative problem solving, original thought, and imagination have become the currency for success in the new world of business . . . and in life.

Your success in getting a promotion, making a sale, raising capital, or reaching your true potential depends on your ability to embrace and nurture your creative potential. Most of us grew up under a promise—one that has turned out to be false. We were led to believe that if we followed the rules, learned a skill, and worked hard we would be pretty much taken care of for life. The promise of a thirty-five-year career at a big company, however, is as extinct as the Oldsmobile, Bear Sterns, and the 8-track tape. Technical skills are important, but they are only one aspect of success in today's ultracompetitive business world. You need to be able to apply those skills in fresh and creative ways in order to drive results in a constantly changing environment.

■ ■ ■

As the economy continues to evolve, businesses are faced with more challenges, increasingly tougher competitors, and less time to react. Dispelling the myths and then harnessing creativity may be the critical success factor for you and your company. Which of these myths were you holding on to? How will you change your thinking in order to change your actions? How will you use your own creativity to make a difference?

APPENDIX B

●

Additional Warm-Up Exercises to Jump-Start Creativity

You've learned how important a creativity warm-up can be. Here are a few more ideas for getting your team ready to tackle any Creativity Challenge:

- **A warm-up challenge.** Take on a small Creativity Challenge that is completely unrelated to your current project, simply to stimulate thinking and get your team in the zone. For example, invent twenty things right now that you could do with a bandana. Or ask, How could we persuade young people not to start smoking? or How could the local flower shop double its sales?

- **Energizers.** Do something fun and physical to get things started. For example, play "the Tower." In this exercise, teams compete to make something out of paper that is tallest (a giraffe, for example).

- **Remote architects exercise.** One person pictures a house in his or her mind. Others ask questions, such as "Is the door in the center or off to one side?" or "Describe the roof." The people who are asking the questions then try to draw the house (given a certain amount of time). Afterward, they compare their drawings to the original idea. People can switch roles and do the activity again. This is a powerful exercise for creating an abstract vision and asking good questions.

- **The magazine story.** Look at a picture in a magazine, art book, or newspaper and create a story about it. Not only the obvious story, but the backstory. The in-between-the-lines. Go around the room and have each person add another layer of detail.

- **Drawing.** Creating visual art is more about seeing than the fine-motor skills needed to produce what you see. Drawing can be a great way to do something physical to get your creative juices flowing. A fun exercise is to print out a page with thirty circles on it and give each team member two minutes to make things out of the circles (clocks, basketballs, faces, and so on). See who can come up with the most creative uses.

- **Logic games.** Play right-brain games to get people thinking in nontraditional ways. Do a puzzle, play Scrabble, or complete a maze. There are dozens of brainteasers available at www.CreativityGeneration.com that can help stimulate your team before directing your creativity toward your own business challenges.

Notes

Introduction

1. Scott Dorsey, founder and CEO, Exact Target, personal interview with Josh Linkner, November 11, 2009.
2. Steven Bean, CEO, Universal Laundry Systems, personal interview with Josh Linkner, October 19, 2009.
3. John Balardo, publisher, Hour Media, personal interview with Josh Linkner, December 9, 2009.
4. Po Bronson and Ashley Merryman, "The Creativity Crisis," *Newsweek,* July 19, 2010, p. 45.

Chapter 1: The Case for Creativity

1. Steve Wynn, remarks made in a live presentation given at the Ernst & Young Entrepreneur of the Year conference, Palm Springs, California, November 2004.
2. Lindsay Edmonds Wickman, "Where Business Meets Jazz," *Chief Learning Officer,* January 2008.
3. Dick Brass, "Microsoft's Creative Destruction," *New York Times,* February 4, 2010.

Chapter 2: Disciplined Dreaming

1. Carlin Flora, "Everyday Creativity," *Psychology Today,* November 5, 2009.
2. Clayton Christensen and Hal Gregersen, "The Innovator's DNA," *Harvard Business Review,* December 21, 2009.
3. Edward de Bono, *Lateral Thinking* (New York: Harper Colophon, 1973).
4. Lori Weiss, television producer and creative director, personal interview with Josh Linkner, October 14, 2009.

Chapter 3: Defining the Creativity Challenge

1. "Disney Buying Pixar for $7.4 billion," MSNBC.com, January 25, 2006.
2. "Rabindranath Tagore Quotes," http://thinkexist.com/quotes/rabindranath_tagore/.
3. Mark Tutton, "Learn the Five Secrets of Innovation," CNN.com, December 1, 2009.

Chapter 4: Driving Curiosity and Awareness

1. Elizabeth Esfahani, "From Tooth to Nail," *Business 2.0*, http://money.cnn.com/magazines/business2/business2_archive/2004/09/01/379531/index.htm, September 1, 2004.
2. Twyla Tharp, *The Creative Habit* (New York: Simon & Schuster, 2006), p. 80.
3. Craig Stull, Phil Myers, and David Meerman Scott, *Tuned In* (Hoboken, NJ: Wiley, 2008).
4. Teresa M. Amabile, "Creativity and Entrepreneurship in the Global Environment," *Centennial Business Summit*, www.hbs.edu/centennial/businesssummit/entrepreneurship/creativity-and-entrepreneurship-in-the-global-environment.html, October 14, 2008.
5. Paul Sloane, "To Be an Innovator, Confront Your Assumptions," innovationtools.com, July 17, 2008.
6. Mihaly Csikszentmihalyi, *Creativity: Flow and the Psychology of Discovery and Invention* (New York: HarperPerennial, 1997), p. 144.

Chapter 5: Gaining the Keys to a Creative Mind and Culture

1. Personal visit to Zappos headquarters by Josh Linkner, Las Vegas, Nevada, July 2009.
2. Dan Gilbert, *ISM's in Action* (Quicken Loans Employee Orientation Manual, reprinted with permission), January 2010.
3. Randall Dunn, head of school, the Roeper School, personal interview with Josh Linkner, November 2009.
4. M. G. Siegler, "How Netflix Fosters a Culture of Success," Web Strategy by Jeremiah Owyang, www.web-strategist.com/blog/2009/08/10/slideshare-how-netflix-fosters-a-culture-of-success/, August 10, 2009.
5. John Balardo, publisher, Hour Media, personal interview with Josh Linkner, December 9, 2009.
6. Chuck Salter, "Failure Doesn't Suck," *Fast Company*, May 1, 2007.
7. Richard Watson, "Everything You Always Wanted to Know About Innovation but Were Afraid to Ask," *Fast Company*, October 7, 2009.

8. Leigh Buchanan, "Innovation: How the Creative Stay Creative," *Inc.*, June 1, 2008.

9. Bill Capodagli and Lynn Jackson, *Innovate the Pixar Way: Business Lessons from the World's Most Creative Corporate Playground* (New York: McGraw-Hill, 2009).

10. Ibid., p. 83.

11. Amjad Hussain, CEO and founder, Silk Route Global, personal interview with Josh Linkner, October 14, 2009.

Chapter 6: Preparing Your Environment to Promote Creative Passion

1. Eva Niewiadomski, founder and CEO, Catalyst Ranch, personal interview with Josh Linkner, October 4, 2009.

2. Personal visit to Google Headquarters by Josh Linkner, Mountain View, California, February 2007.

3. Eric Lefkowski, founder of Interworkings, Inc.; Echo Global Logistics, Inc.; MediaBank, LLC; and Groupon.com, Inc.; personal interview with Josh Linkner, November 19, 2009.

4. Carl Woideck, *Charlie Parker: His Music and Life* (Ann Arbor: University of Michigan Press, 1998).

5. Craig Erlich, CEO, Pulse 220, personal interview with Josh Linkner, August 13, 2009.

6. David Womack, "Project Platypus: Reinventing Product Development at Mattel, an Interview with Ivy Ross," *Gain: AIGA Journal of Business and Design,* March 6, 2003.

Chapter 7: Discovering the Ways of Creativity

1. Jon Citrin, founder and CEO, the Citrin Group, personal interview with Josh Linkner, October 15, 2009.

2. Dan Gilbert, founder and chairman, Quicken Loans; majority owner, Cleveland Cavaliers, personal interview with Josh Linkner, September 15, 2009.

3. Craig Stull, Phil Myers, and David Meerman Scott, *Tuned In* (Hoboken, NJ: Wiley, 2008).

4. Andrew S. Grove, *Only the Paranoid Survive: How to Exploit the Crisis Points That Challenge Every Company* (New York: Crown Business, 1999).

5. "George de Mestral," Invention at Play, http://invention.smithsonian.org/centerpieces/iap/inventors_dem.html, n.d.

6. Joseph Michelli, *The Starbucks Experience: Five Principals for Turning Ordinary into Extraordinary* (New York: McGraw-Hill, 2006).

7. Harvey Kanter, CEO and president, Moosejaw Mountaineering and Backcountry Travel, Inc., personal interview with Josh Linkner, October 13, 2009.

8. Bethany McLean, "Diamonds Go Designer," *Fortune,* CNNMoney.com, November 2, 2007.

Chapter 8: Generating Creative Sparks

1. Eric Maisel, *Coaching the Artist Within: Advice for Writers, Actors, Visual Artists, and Musicians from America's Foremost Creativity Coach* (Novato, CA: New World Library, 2005).
2. Paul Sloane, *The Leader's Guide to Lateral Thinking Skills: Unlocking the Creativity and Innovation in You and Your Team* (London: Kogan Page, 2006).
3. Ross Sanders, executive director, Bizdom U Entrepreneurial Academy, personal interview with Josh Linkner, December 4, 2009.
4. Ellen Florian, "The Money Machines," *Fortune,* CNNMoney.com, July 26, 2004.
5. Ernie Perich, founder and CEO, Perich+Partners Advertising, personal interview with Josh Linkner, November 25, 2009.

Chapter 9: Igniting the Sparks of Creativity

1. Institute of Leadership & Management, *Managing Creativity and Innovation in the Workplace Super Series, Fifth Edition* (United Kingdom: Pergamon Flexible Learning, 2007).
2. Post Foods, LLC, "Post Heritage," www.postcereals.com/post_heritage, 2008.
3. William C. Taylor and Polly G. LaBarre, *Mavericks at Work* (New York: Morrow, 2006).
4. Brian Gillespie, chief creative officer, BarCom, personal interview with Josh Linkner, December 12, 2009.
5. Allison Stein Wellner, "A Perfect Brainstorm," *Inc.,* October 1, 2003.
6. Arthur B. VanGundy, "Brain Writing for New Product Ideas: An Alternative to Brainstorming," *Journal of Consumer Marketing*, 1993, *1*(2), 67–74.
7. Steven Rogelberg, Janet Barnes-Farrell and Charles Lowe, "The Stepladder Technique," *Journal of Applied Psychology*, 1992, *77*(5), 730–737.

Chapter 10: Bringing Your Ideas to Life

1. William C. Taylor and Polly G. LaBarre, *Mavericks at Work* (New York: Morrow, 2006).

2. Sir Richard Branson, *Screw It, Let's Do It: Lessons in Life and Business* (London: Virgin Books, 2010).

3. Evan Weiner, president, the Edward C. Levy Company, personal interview with Josh Linkner, January 27, 2010.

4. Kerry Capell, "Zara Thrives by Breaking All the Rules," *Bloomberg Businessweek*, October 9, 2008.

Acknowledgments

A work of this nature is never a solo act. I am truly blessed to have the support, friendship, and guidance of so many people. Their confidence in me allowed me to bring this book to life, and I owe them immeasurable gratitude.

Thanks to Karen Murphy, my passionate editor from Jossey-Bass; Esmond Harmsworth, my thoughtful literary agent from Zachary, Shuster, Harmsworth; and the amazing coaching duo of Nick and Nikki Morgan from Public Words. They each pushed me beyond my comfort zone to make this a better book.

Thanks to my partner and friend, Jordan Broad, who is helping make the world a more creative planet through his dynamic leadership of the Institute for Applied Creativity.

Thank you to all the ePrizers from the past and present, who not only helped me build an amazing company but also truly helped create a family. I have learned so much from you and am especially grateful for your passion, creativity, and drive.

I am so fortunate to have had amazing business partners and mentors throughout my career. Special thanks to Dan Gilbert, Brian Hermelin, Gary Shiffman, Steve Friedman, Phil Elkus, Alon Kaufman, Arthur Weiss, Bruce Seyburn, and Jack Rosenzweig. I was only able to achieve success by standing on the shoulders of these giants.

So many friends contributed to the launch of this book, both directly and in spirit. Thank you to Craig and Renee Erlich, David Farbman, Juergen Rochert, Mark D'Andreta, Rob Holloway, Paul

Glomski, Tom Proctor, John Caputo, Rich and Jeff Sloan, Neil Rosenzweig, Tia Kouchary, Alesya Opelt, Jeff Davidson, Pete Davis, Doyle Mosher, Matt Mosher, Jim Rosenthal, Alan Strickstein, Jackie Trepanier, Jen Grey, Sagar Parvataneni, Bob Marsh, Gary Shuman, Kaiser Yang, Ted Paff, Patrick Doran, Robb Lippitt, Jonathan Liebman, Guymon Ensley, Jeff Ponders, Ibrihim Jones, Phil Lesky, Ivan Frank, Matt Wise, Kathy Hoffman, Jon Citrin, Gabe Karp, Craig Sprinkle, and John Balardo. Also, thanks to all the members of YPO International for many years of friendship and learning.

A gigantic thank you to the two hundred people I interviewed for this book. Your contributions made the text come to life, and I am so grateful for your insight and wisdom.

And finally, thank you to my zany family: Noah, Chloe, Ethan, Sarah and Nick, Renita, Robert, Monica, Mickey, Nancy and Doug, Erika and Aaron, Lev and Deb, Michael and Joe, and all the rest of the gang. Your support and love enabled me to make my dreams a reality.

About the Author

J osh Linkner is an entrepreneur, jazz musician, venture capitalist, speaker, and author. He is the founder and chairman of ePrize, the largest interactive promotion agency in the world. ePrize has produced digital promotions for seventy-four of the top one hundred brands across thirty-seven countries and has won dozens of awards.

Josh was named the Ernst & Young Entrepreneur of the Year (2004), Crain's 40 under 40 (2003), Automation Alley's CEO of the Year (2005), and Detroit Executive of the Year (2009). He is a highly sought-after keynote speaker and is a frequent source for comment among top business, technology, and marketing media. He has been featured in the *Wall Street Journal, Fast Company, Advertising Age, Entrepreneur, Adweek*, and *Inc*.

Josh lives in Detroit, Michigan, and continues to improvise both in the business world and in smoky jazz clubs. To follow Josh's blog or learn more, visit www.CreativityGeneration.com.

Index